—

Praise for *Behind the Screen*

—

"From the moment you contemplate taking an audition to the moments after it's finished, *Behind the Screen* is the ultimate guide for your audition journey. The author's honest and straightforward approach makes this book accessible for anyone undertaking the audition process. It's a must have!"

— TODD COPE
Principal Clarinet, l'Orchestre symphonique de Montréal

"A perfect companion for aspiring clarinetists! Totally recommend!"

— BORIS ALLAKHVERDYAN
Principal Clarinet, Los Angeles Philharmonic

"*Behind the Screen* gives the reader a seasoned veteran's view of audition preparation that would normally take a lifetime to learn. This performance planning guide gives everyone an exclusive insight into the thoughtful process of a top-tier clarinetist. Ralph Skiano's expressive and concise narrative of the audition preparation process can be extremely useful for getting ready for any performance at all levels."

— RICHIE HAWLEY
Professor of Clarinet at the Shepherd School of Music, Rice University
Former Principal Clarinet, Cincinnati Symphony

About the Author

Ralph Skiano currently serves as Principal Clarinetist of the Detroit Symphony Orchestra after serving in the same position in the Cincinnati Symphony, the Richmond Symphony, and the Des Moines Metro Opera. He has also appeared as guest Principal Clarinetist of the Seattle Symphony and the Cleveland Orchestra.

Mr. Skiano has served on the faculty of the Cincinnati College-Conservatory of Music, and at the Schools of Music at James Madison University and the College of William and Mary. His students currently have positions in several professional military bands and orchestras in this country.

Acknowledgments

I'd like to thank two people for their gifts of time, energy, and inspiration in my musical and professional life.

I'll never underestimate the impact we each might have on young lives because of the impact that Marguerite Levin had on me as a young clarinetist. She opened my eyes to the world of music, teaching me the skills I needed to experience it at a high level in high school. She instilled in me a deep love and appreciation of the power and depth of music, which would have enriched my life even if I hadn't pursued a musical career.

In the same way, I now know the importance of finding a generous and enthusiastic teacher and mentor as you continue to develop later in life. I found that in Richie Hawley, who inspired me from the stage in the Cincinnati Symphony Orchestra, and who helped unlock excitement and expression in my playing during my time studying with him at CCM. His practical advice and musical guidance are the foundation of the methods that eventually helped me to find a place in the music world, and many of the ideas described in this book were inspired by him.

ISBN 978-1-7352857-2-6

Book design by Greg Skiano
Edited by Megan Krone, Ralph and Peggy Skiano
Cover photo by Hart Hollman

www.ralphskiano.com

BEHIND THE SCREEN

Behind the Screen

A Winner's Guide to Preparing Your Next Audition

BY RALPH SKIANO

Preface

I've loved music my whole life, and I realized early on that, if I wanted to make a life playing in an orchestra, I'd have to learn to deal with a very difficult and often demoralizing experience... *taking an audition.*

The competition on the audition circuit was intense, but despite the odds, early in my career, I secured tenured Principal Clarinet positions in several orchestras. How? By staying curious and by constantly evaluating my preparation methods to make them more effective and (dare I say) more fun!

While it's true that I've won a few auditions, I've also lost many. After each, I would often forget the lessons I had learned while preparing. I would forget the pressure of the day and the stress leading up to it. I would forget how challenging it was to prepare a long list of excerpts while working and living my life. I found myself regularly underestimating the challenges of the experience.

I wrote this book mostly as a letter to my future self: a "treasure map" back to the most helpful mindsets, routines, and processes that I developed over the last 20 years of auditioning for orchestras of all sizes. Now, as my auditioning days are coming to a close, my hope is that you can gain some ideas from these pages to improve your next audition.

I firmly believe there is no magic formula or schedule for audition preparation. Every musician is different, and each audition is unique. Some people "wing it," while others stick to demanding schedules for weeks leading up to an audition. I've never been one to "wing" much of anything, so I always encourage my students (and myself) to develop a plan that will allow them to be very prepared, very inspired, very relaxed, and, most challenging of all, very detached from outcomes. If you're looking for strategies to achieve these goals, you've come to the right place.

This book is for:

- The student in college who has never taken an audition.
- Someone with a few professional auditions under their belt looking to improve their performance under pressure.
- The person playing in a small orchestra and looking to move up.
- Anyone seeking ideas for playing this game more successfully and creatively.

Even though the examples I use in this book are clarinet-specific, anyone can benefit from the concepts and apply them to their instrument of choice.

This is a flexible guide. You can read it cover to cover or skip to the parts that work best for you. This guide is not prescriptive. If something says it should take three days and you only have one: Adapt. Evolving your process is essential. If you always prepare the same way, you either did it perfectly the first time (not likely) or you are not really learning.

· TABLE OF CONTENTS ·

CHAPTER 1

PREPARE

Apply for the position and organize the tools you will need to succeed.

Suggested time: 1–3 days

Here you will find information about making the decision to take an audition, how to apply, what kinds of materials you should assemble before you begin to practice, and how to make a plan for your physical and mental health.

Give me six hours to
chop down a tree
and I will spend the first four
sharpening the axe.

ABRAHAM LINCOLN

Decide and Commit

If you *are* going to take the audition, decide and commit to it NOW instead of waiting until the week before it happens (when nobody feels ready). You'll be more focused and serious in your preparation, and you won't be constantly giving yourself an excuse to not work as hard as you can.

How much time do you need to prepare?

How much time you need to prepare depends on where you are in life and what kind of an audition you are taking.

If you're a student, plan for 6–8 weeks. If you are playing a job already, I'd say 4–6 weeks. If you've been out on the audition trail for a while and are already in great shape, maybe 2–4 weeks. If you are a "seasoned" professional and haven't taken an audition in years, plan for 6–8 weeks. It's harder than you probably remember!

It's important to be respectful of the time and effort it will take to prepare, but don't be scared off if you don't have the exact number of weeks you think you need. Only *you* will be able to decide what you need to be confident and compelling. Just use the time you have in an organized and deliberate way to make the most of it.

Is this an audition you should take?

Ask yourself two questions: Is this a job you really want? And, do you have the time to adequately prepare? You probably know the answer to both

questions. Don't audition just for the experience of auditioning without doing the right kind of preparation. It's expensive, and you're setting yourself up for disappointment. On the other hand, don't be afraid just because you think you lack experience, or you think the job is too big for you at this point in your life. If you are practicing hard and are getting good feedback from the people you trust, it's time to get out there and throw your hat in the ring. You can learn on the job quickly! As one of my favorite teachers says, "You can't win the lottery if you don't buy a ticket!" Maybe it's time for you to *buy a ticket!*

Apply

The application process is simple. Contact the orchestra to express your interest. Usually, you will need a short cover letter or email stating you'd like to apply for the position and that you've enclosed or attached your resume. Your one-page resume should include all relevant performance experience, prominent teachers, and any recent audition final rounds. At first your resume may be full of school awards and festivals, but as you get older and gain more experience, you should try to replace those items on your resume with more professional experiences.

How do people get pre-advanced?

Pre-advancement varies from orchestra to orchestra. Sometimes a limited number of candidates may be invited to start directly in the semi-finals or finals. In some situations the orchestra musicians might have the ability to invite colleagues. In others, the

Music Director might extend such invitations. Some orchestras have a standing policy about qualifications for a candidate to be pre-advanced, such as if someone already has a tenured position in an International Conference of Symphony and Orchestra Musician (ICSOM) orchestra. And of course, some orchestras simply make every candidate start in the preliminaries.

Reasons you might request a pre-advancement include playing a similar position in another orchestra of similar or larger size, making finals in a previous audition for the same orchestra, making finals in other large orchestra auditions consistently, or having played an extended time as a substitute in the position being auditioned.

If you feel you can make the case for why you should be pre-advanced at the audition, I suggest you write if the committee will consider placing you in the semi-finals. The worst that can happen is that they say no. You've got nothing to lose by asking.

Relationships in the music world matter, so even if you are an undergraduate student, foster a supportive and professional approach to your work and to your colleagues now. The relationships you make at each step in your journey will become important in ways you can't anticipate. Be the type of person and colleague that you'd want to have in *your* orchestra or university some day. You never know which of your friends might become professional orchestral players, conductors, artistic administrators, professors, deans, or festival directors. People will remember you, for better or worse.

What if they say you're not invited?

In some instances, your request to audition might be denied. I've heard stories of people showing up to an audition even without an invitation and winning, but it's not something that happens often. You can ask the committee to reconsider, perhaps with a recommendation from someone who might have some influence with a musician on the committee, but this also rarely works.

Should you play a live preliminary or make a tape?

Some orchestras offer the choice of playing a preliminary round by tape or playing live. Deciding which option is best for you can be tricky, especially when one option costs significantly more.

If you are not sure you have a good chance to win and/or money is tight, consider making a tape. If you make a tape, prepare as though it is a live audition. Use the best possible audio quality you can afford (i.e. studio quality). Make sure your sound is beautiful and there is audible dynamic contrast. Do not adjust the volume of individual tracks. Soft excerpts should sound soft and loud ones should sound loud. Recorded preliminaries need to sound like you are playing live and must represent your very best playing, because the committee will expect you had time to make multiple recordings.

However, if you are prepared, sounding your best, feel confident, and have the budget to do so, I recommend playing live. Playing live ensures you'll be heard as you are and removes the variable of recording quality from the assessment of your audition. Will the committee be more forgiving of a live round vs a tape round? Probably not. It still has to be great playing!

Book Your Travel

Once you've been invited to audition, commit. Book your travel and post copies of your travel reservations to your computer, mirror, television or anywhere else you might need a reminder. Take a screen shot of the flight information and make it your "unlock" image on your phone to remind you of your goals and to keep you from wasting time.

When I plan my travel for an audition, there are several important factors to consider.

Location: If the conditions are relatively similar to my home, I plan on arriving the day before I need to play. If there will be a significant shift in climate or altitude, I try to arrive two or more days early to give myself a fighting chance at having a working reed on audition day.

Length of stay: I always plan to advance at the audition. It can end up being more expensive, but it helps my confidence to plan for success. Then my back-up plan, if I don't advance, is to try to enjoy exploring a new city! Of course, when it doesn't go my way, it's sometimes a long, dreary few days in an unfamiliar place. The tradeoff is worth the feeling that it's possible to go all the way when I am preparing.

Accommodations: Where you choose to stay during the audition might have an impact on your performance. I always consider proximity to the hall, privacy, and cost. I will preface these recommendations by saying that I do not deal well with stress and anxiety by making small talk or visiting with friends or relatives. I don't even feel comfortable around my own family when I am worried about a performance. You may not feel the same way, and so these recommendations may not be right for you. That's okay!

Hotel: I try to choose a hotel that is about a twenty-minute walk from the hall. Hotels any closer will be jammed with clarinetists all practicing Daphnis at full speed and volume, which is my worst nightmare. In addition, the walk to and from the hotel helps me manage my nerves. I don't like to rely on public transportation to get to the hall, because I don't want the added stress of timing and delays. Rental cars are also not ideal because of stressful traffic and the headache of finding parking when it isn't provided.

Airbnb: I use the same criteria as above, except I'm clear with the owner that I will be making noise in the unit. In an Airbnb it's usually a safe bet you won't hear other clarinetists playing.

Friends or family: It may work for some people to have others care for them and support them during the audition process, and staying with family or friends might save you some money. However, I find the time alone better for maintaining focus, so I avoid this option.

Assemble Your Study Materials

There will be a lot of information in this section, but the work shouldn't eat up too much of your preparation time. Limit it to only a few days if you can, but try to complete the assembly of all of your study and practice materials before you move on to the next phase. *Do not cut corners*. The more organized and meticulous you are in this phase, the less stress you will feel in the following phases. Assembling all of these materials will make you much more efficient and effective over the course of the next few weeks. This is one place I often see people cutting corners. They don't assemble the listening list fully, or they don't finish the audition book before they start practicing and then later, they feel frazzled and disorganized.

For this book, I will use a real example of the Principal Clarinet audition for the Detroit Symphony Orchestra in 2014 *(pictured opposite)*.

Step 1: Make your audition book

First, assemble and organize your parts. I strongly suggest you use double-sided photocopies of unmarked (if possible) full parts, unless the orchestra sends out copies of the excerpts they want to hear. Do not use parts from excerpt books or cheap imitation parts from the International Music Score Library Project (IMSLP) if they aren't exactly like the real printed versions. I've seen many versions on IMSLP that contain mistakes. You can order parts from a publishing company or ask around. Your teachers and colleagues might have copies of what you need.

I use unmarked parts because I like to start fresh each time, looking for new ideas about phrasing that inspire and excite me now, instead of trying to churn out the "perfect" execution of the "right" way to play something every year. Start creating your library of unmarked parts now (digital or hard copies). It will make each audition preparation easier and will be a very valuable resource moving forward.

I make a separate book (at a copy shop like FedEx Office: black back, clear front, coil binding) for each audition. I keep them all with my markings in them as a reference for future auditions.

In every book, I also include the following:

- Cover page: Audition repertoire list from the orchestra.
- My Direction of Intention: One page to guide my thoughts and intentions on audition day. When nerves creep in, I read this over and over to calm and focus my mind. A worksheet to create your own is included in *Quick Guides* at the end of this book.
- A few blank pages at the end for notes.
- There are a few other sheets in the *Quick Guides* at the end of this book that you might like to include that might help you navigate audition day and help you to track your experiences for future auditions.

If you don't mind the additional expense, make a second copy of the book for mock auditions. It makes it easier for someone to give feedback if they also have a copy of the music while listening.

Detroit Symphony Orchestra
Principal Clarinet Audition Repertoire
March 2014

I. <u>**SOLO REPERTOIRE**</u>

MOZART	Concerto in A, K: 622, Mvts. I & II
COPLAND	Clarinet Concerto, cadenza

II. <u>**ORCHESTRAL EXCERPTS**</u>

BEETHOVEN	Symphony No. 4
	Symphony No. 6
	Symphony No. 8
BRAHMS	Symphony No. 3
KODALY	Dances of Galanta
MENDELSSOHN	Midsummer Night's Dream, Scherzo
	Symphony No. 3, Mvts. II & IV
RACHMANINOFF	Symphony No. 2, Mvt. III
RAVEL	Daphnis and Chloe, Suite No. 2
	Bolero
RESPIGHI	Pines of Rome
RIMSKY-KORSAKOV	Capriccio Espagnole
	Scheherazade
SCHUBERT	Symphony No. 8 (Unfinished)
SHOSTAKOVICH	Symphony No. 1
	Symphony No. 9, Mvts. II & III
SIBELIUS	Symphony No. 1, Mvts. I (Opening solo) & III
STRAUSS	Don Juan
STRAVINSKY	Firebird Suite (1919)
TCHAIKOVSKY	Symphony No. 6, Mvt. I

III. <u>**POSSIBLE SIGHT-READING**</u>

Step 2: Make your listening list

Once you have your audition book, it's time to acquire recordings and chop them into individual excerpts for laser-like efficiency in study. THIS IS CRUCIAL! It makes studying easier and faster, so you can do it more often. It helps to solidify the choreography of your mind in the actual audition: Your mind will more likely be filled with music in the right tempo, at the right pitch, and in the right character. Trust me. *Do this step.*

Create a playlist in your media player that contains your entire excerpt library as you do this work. Then, make a separate playlist for each audition and title it with the orchestra name (e.g. "Detroit Symphony Principal Clarinet").

Each excerpt should be edited in the same way:

- Fade into the music a few bars before the solo (try and be intentional about this because it will be the few bars you hear in your head before you play in the audition).
- Fade out at the end of the solo.
- Add 3–4 seconds of silence.
- Adjust for volume to avoid extremely loud excerpts in your list. I always found I needed to reduce the levels of Capriccio Espagnol so as to not go deaf when studying.

Once the list is done, keep it with you at all times. This can be accomplished by simply creating a playlist on your phone. Listen every time you get in the car, when you clean the house, as you fall asleep, when you wake up in the morning, as you get ready for your day, travel to work or school, walk the dog... The point is LISTEN, and if you can, form habits that ensure you listen a lot.

As you look through the list from the DSO, you might be wondering, "How do I handle a list that doesn't specify specific excerpts?" For now, focus your attention on any standard excerpts from this repertoire. For help figuring out what would qualify as "standard", ask friends or teachers. I will address the question of preparing full parts in *Chapter 2* of this book.

Audio Editing Software

I've used *Audacity* or *Sound Studio*, but there are many options for sound editing software. *Audacity* is free!

Fade in	Intro	The Excerpt	Fade out	Silence
2 seconds	A few bars		2 seconds	3 seconds

Step 3: Create your "audition mode" daily warmup

When preparing for an audition, it's important to establish a daily routine that will ground you, give you confidence in your approach to excerpts, and undo the negative effects of long hours of practice (e.g. lack of flexibility, hearing intonation as "clarinet pitch," improper use of air). I rotate which instrument I warm up on to stay comfortable on each (A/Bb/Eb/Bcl). In *my* warmup, I include technical work, articulation work, ear training, flexibility exercises, dynamic range exercises, and high attacks. I follow my instincts and try to be creative in addressing my current weaknesses through these exercises. I also re-evaluate and edit this warmup routine throughout the preparation to be sure it is serving its purpose.

I always do a daily warmup, even on the day of the audition. It should only take 20–25 minutes. Warming up for me is about compartmentalizing techniques and giving them all of my focus for a relatively short amount of time. Then these techniques are more easily incorporated into the repertoire I'm practicing. I address three basic skills every day: fingers (and air at the same time), articulation (fast and medium), and intonation. When I am in audition mode, I also use some excerpts as a part of my warmup, and I force myself to play them on whatever reed I first pull out of my case. I don't want my Shostakovich 9 or my Beethoven 6 to be dependent on my having found the ideal reed on audition day, so I try to play them as part of my warmup every day (as you will see in the articulation section).

Fingers: Any technical studies would work for this, but I suggest finding something you can complete in under 15 minutes. The goal is to blow like you are playing the most beautiful long tones (even at fast tempi), while also focusing on playing with incredible evenness and relaxation. Watch your finger movement, pay attention to tension in your shoulders, make sure you are not biting, create wonderful resonance, and treat this as a meditation about how clarinet should be played under ideal circumstances. This should be pleasurable and grounding. I'm pretty unimaginative and old-school in my choices, but rotating them gives me variety:

- Baermann Book 3 scales and arpeggios
- Klosé scales and arpeggios
- JeanJean Vade-Mecum

Articulation: Articulation is one area where I have always struggled. It causes me a fair amount of anxiety, so I've developed a series of exercises to give me the confidence I need under pressure. You may not need everything I use, but pay attention to articulation in some way each day.

I want to be comfortable with rapid articulation for Beethoven 4 and Bartered Bride (144–152), as well as the medium-fast triplet articulations of Beethoven 6 and Shostakovich 9 (112–120). My exercises for these are on the following pages.

Intonation: Playing in tune with yourself is crucial, especially in a big hall with a lot of reverb. I do two daily exercises with a drone: Kincaid Scales, and Singing Intervals (both appear on the following pages).

Articulation 1: Rapid

The following are a series of my daily exercises to maintain rapid articulation. The goal is to minimize tongue pressure and tongue movement while maintaining air support. **I am trying to train my body to relax as the speed increases, rather than becoming tense** (which is the body's normal reaction).

Rhythmic Hairpin: Do this on C, D, E, F, G, etc. Play with legato articulation.

Slurred and articulated pentatonic scales at 160–164: Keep moving the starting note up chromatically.

Slurred and articulated one-octave scales at 150–154: Keep moving starting note up chromatically.

Slurred and articulated two-octave scales at 140-144: Keep moving starting note up.

Follow with Beethoven 4 slurred, then articulated:

– Two measures at a time at 160–164

– Three or four measures at a time at 150–154

– Complete at 140–144

Articulation 2: Triplets

To prepare myself for playing the first movement of Beethoven 6 and the third movement of Shostakovich 9, I play one or two pages of the Baermann arpeggios (quarter note = 112–120), but I play them in triplets, like this one in C major (the first printed tie becomes two eighth note triplets):

Minimize tongue movement and pressure while maintaining air support. Find a consistent voicing, maintain a bouncing and even quality, and avoid biting. Follow with Beethoven 6 first movement and Shostakovich 9 third movement.

Intonation 1: Kincaid Scales

I will always be grateful to my good friend Brian Gordon of the Phoenix Symphony for showing me this first exercise: the Kincaid Scales. He does them in all twelve keys.

I always play these scales with a drone. This isn't just about intonation but phrasing as well. Use each resting point as a moment to gather musical energy to carry the line to the next resting point. I like to think of them as an orchestral solo. On the way down, I breathe after each fermata to practice attacks without being sharp.

Intonation 2: Singing Intervals

I use this exercise in all twelve keys with a drone to focus on resonance and relaxation in upward intervals while maintaining good pitch and support in the descending line at the end. Strive for a very smooth, vocal and relaxed upward interval (think Strauss), and don't bite on the way down.

Step 4: Plan for physical and mental toughness

Consider now if you'd like to investigate mental and physical toughness training of some kind, and if so, commit to a daily practice geared toward training your mind and body.

Physical: Physical toughness is fairly straightforward. Essentially, you should decide how you will move your body every day to address the physical strains the audition preparation process will cause. This could be jogging, lifting weights, walking, doing yoga, or whatever you feel like doing to make sure you aren't ignoring your body. Staying even mildly active will help you to deal with stress and anxiety. Try to move your body every day in some way.

Mental: Your unconscious mind is always working. Make it work for you, not against you.

Early in my professional career, I became aware that my subconscious mind was working all of the time, and if I didn't actively train it to help me, it would probably undermine all of my hard work in the practice room. I have always experienced anxiety in competitions or auditions, but I started feeling anxiety even at work as I became very sensitive to every facial expression I saw on the faces of my colleagues while playing in the orchestra. I could hear their voices in my head saying, "Wow, THAT was really out of tune" or "I can't believe we hired HIM" or "How can he honestly play that passage like THAT?" It was debilitating.

In the years since, I've found the following training methods extremely helpful. Whichever mental training you choose, try to do it daily. Yes, this counts as practicing!

Meditation

It seems like every author who writes about health and wellness suggests mindfulness training as a part of their regimen. Whether this helps you win auditions or not, it's going to impact your life in positive ways.

I wanted to create a daily practice I would carry on long after the audition was done. I started by using an app called *Headspace*. This app teaches mindfulness and meditation through a series of graduated, guided exercises. There are specific programs that deal with all kinds of struggles, such as anxiety, depression, gratitude, patience, and priorities. It's great for someone who is new to this ancient practice and needs some guidance. There are also other apps (e.g. Calm) and resources that can support a meditation practice for beginners or experienced practitioners. Find something that works for you!

In the beginning, most programs encourage you to become very aware of your body and breath. They guide you through the skill of placing your attention in different places intentionally and show you ways to deal with distracting thoughts. For me, after some practice, I feel my mind becomes more resilient. During auditions, the negative voices that are always so intrusive show up less often, and when they do show up, I don't entertain them or get swept away by them.

Meditation has proven helpful to me in the orchestra as well. Each *Headspace* meditation begins by grounding me in the present, including "feeling my weight in the chair". This practice has become helpful to me in orchestra performances when I am anxiously waiting to play an exposed solo. It takes up some mental "bandwidth" and helps block out intrusive and unhelpful thinking. I only have room to think about two or MAYBE

three things simultaneously: feeling my weight in the chair, counting my rests, and playing with expression!

When you are pressed for time, it can be hard to feel like spending time practicing meditation contributes to your practice plan, but it is audition practice, and it pays off in big ways when you are consistent with it.

Visualization

Much has been written about the use of visualization, and I won't repeat that work here. Don Greene has written extensively about visualization in auditions, and *The Bulletproof Musician* (a useful blog) has some great articles about it as well. If you are interested, I'd start with their work.

I use visualization in three specific ways:

First, I practice visualization when I am fatigued or traveling as I would practice anything on my instrument. It can be a substitute for practice time. I visualize playing through passages and imagine how it feels, then I repeat. Sometimes visualized practice feels just as productive as the real thing!

Second, during the final phase of preparation, I visualize my ideal audition round. Engaging as many senses as possible, I close my eyes and imagine playing through each excerpt with all of the "choreography" I have established: getting the tempo, thinking of the character, taking the right breath, playing with my most beautiful tone, taking expressive risks, and enjoying myself in the process.

Third, on audition day, when my nerves might be getting the best of me, I do a simple visualization where I picture myself walking off the stage, having just played, with a giant smile on my face and the feeling that I just had a blast making music! Then, I rewind the tape and play it again. I try to do that ten times in a row. This reduces some of the pressure to play perfectly and reminds me of how much I love making music and sharing it with people. This is great to use in the warmup room because it saves my chops and keep me fresh and mentally engaged.

I do a simple visualization where I picture myself walking off the stage, having just played, with a giant smile on my face and the feeling that I just had a blast making music!

Self-hypnosis

I like self-hypnosis because it feels like a targeted and personalized attack on my specific insecurities and anxieties. For me, it involves a pre-recorded and carefully scripted message that lasts about twenty minutes. If I listen to it daily, it has a very noticeable effect on my confidence.

If you want to try out self-hypnosis, there is an app called *Hypnosis for Musicians*. It has settings for preset messages that might be helpful, and it's very easy to use.

I started by seeing a few different therapists who practiced hypnosis. I found their services helpful, but too general. I wanted something more in-depth, so I searched, believing I'd find something someone else had created that would work well for me. I downloaded and read many scripts. Then I downloaded a bunch of hypnosis recordings to see if I could find something that would meet my needs. Nothing fit. Either they didn't address my specific anxieties, or they inadvertently led me to develop new anxieties about things that never bothered me before!

I decided to create my own script and my own recording. Although it took time, energy, and research to create, it became an incredibly easy training method. Once it was recorded, I simply listened to my tape once a day.

To create my own script, I used a variety of resources, including downloaded hypnosis scripts, some of Don Greene's writings, some articles from *The Bullet-Proof Musician*, some quotes and advice from my teachers, and some things from the book *The Relaxed Musician: A 14-Day Program for Optimal Mental Preparation* by Dr. Diana Allan. I also borrowed a recording of a friend's hypnosis session with their therapist to get an idea of how to pace my speech and how to inflect my voice to induce a trance. Then I bought an audio track I thought would make a good background. I chose a track called *"Inner Mind,"* created by Dr. Jeffrey Thompson in his *Gamma Meditation System*. With an audio editor, some vocal processing, and a bit of reverb here and there, I came up with something that works very well for me.

Should you do the same? Maybe, but start by looking into some of the resources mentioned above, and then contact a professional to help. If your subconscious mind is wrestling with deeper issues, a professional might be necessary to really be effective.

Note: If you do seek out professional hypnosis services, please be cautious about well-meaning therapists that seek to help you find the "zone" or "flow state". Being in the "zone" is something many musicians experience, but it's not something you can just conjure up when you want it... at least not reliably. If it happens, GREAT! Enjoy it! However, for me, getting in the "zone" is more like trying to fall asleep... the harder you try to make it happen, the less likely you'll succeed. You need tools to help you deal with the moments you are *not* in the zone. That's really when you need your mental training!

My Daily Plan

- Daily 5–10 minute meditation in the morning
- Nightly 20 minute self-hypnosis
- Visualization when traveling and in the warmup room

My Audition Plan

- Guided 20 minute meditation or self-hypnosis to use in the warmup room

1

Meditation

Easy and self-guided

Can be short

General in approach

2

Visualization

Not guided

Performance-specific

Short or long time period

3

Self-Hypnosis

Powerful

Upfront investment of time

Easy to use

Step 5: *Create your practice chart*

Now that you have your listening list, your audition book, your warmup, and your mental and physical plans, it's time to organize everything on a chart. A practice chart helps to better plan my time, stay accountable to myself for the goals I set, and understand why certain things are or are not working well on any given day. I can look for clues about how my preparation affects my performance, observe patterns, and alter my path if I think my current plan isn't serving me well.

I use a spreadsheet for my practice chart. Across the top, I label the columns with the days of the week. The first group of rows track my daily tasks (physical exercise and meditation). The next group of rows track my warmups (I rotate daily between A and Bb). The next row(s) track my other responsibilities (in this case, just music for the Richmond Symphony). After that, I include one row for each individual excerpt or concerto movement. At the bottom, if the audition doesn't request specific excerpts, I add a row for "full parts practice", which is basically any music not specifically included on this chart.

In *Chapter 2*, I will explain how I color-code the excerpts, dividing them into a rotation. For now, the important thing is to have them on the chart, so you can mark what you've worked on each day.

I've used paper charts and I've created charts on my iPad. I like both. The paper version is easier to use and feels more like I'm actually studying. The digital version has much more capabilities with colors, emojis, fonts, and the ability to insert notes to your future self about what to focus on in your next session. It also tracks long term trends and goals more easily because it can be infinitely long. This also makes it ideal for charting when the audition list is very long. You can see that this paper version is very small to fit it all on one page, so I would likely use a digital version for this list. Try both methods and see which one works better for you!

I find it helpful to use markings in the cells to indicate what I did exactly (rather than just checking them off). I use the symbols below when marking my charts. They will appear in examples throughout the rest of this book and are probably self-explanatory.

Example Practice Chart Markings

X	Practiced
XX	Practiced a lot
90	Top tempo was 90bpm
R	Recorded
L	Listened
RL	Recorded and listened
RLX	Recorded, listened, & practiced
PA	Played along
V	Visualized
:-)	Went well
:-(	Went poorly
:-/	Went okay
B84	Did Baermann Scales at 84
K100	Klosé Scales at 100
JJ110	JeanJean Vade-Mecum at 110

My DSO Audition Practice Chart

	M	T	W	Th	F	S	Su	M	T	W	Th	F	S	Su
Exercise														
Meditation														
Warmup	A	Bb	A	Bb	A	Bb	A	Bb						
Fingers														
Articulation														
Intonation														
Richmond Rep														
Mozart I														
Mozart II														
Copland														
Beethoven 4 II														
Beethoven 4 IV														
Beethoven 6 I														
Beethoven 6 IIA														
Beethoven 6 IIB														
Beethoven 6 III														
Beethoven 8 trio														
Brahms 3 IA														
Brahms 3 IB														
Brahms 3 II														
Galanta I														
Galanta middle														
Galanta end														
Mend Scherzo														
Mend 3 II														
Mend 3 IV														
Rach 2														
Daphnis Noodles														
Daphnis Last 2														
Bolero														
Pines														
Capriccio I														
Capriccio III														
Capriccio IV														
Scheherazade II														
Scheherazade IIIa														
Scheherazade IIIb														
Scheherazade IIIc														
Scheherazade IIId														
Scheherazade IV														
Schubert 8														
Shost 1 Ia														
Shost 1 Ib														
Shost 1 Ic														
Shost 1 Id														
Shost 1 II														
Shost 1 IV all														
Shost 9 II														
Shost 9 III														
Sibelius 1 I														
Sibelius 1 IIIa														
Sibelius 1 IIIb														
Don Juan														
Firebird														
Tchaik 6 Ia														
Tchaik 6 Ib														
Tchaik 6 Ic														
Full Parts Practice														

Physical & Mental Work

Use words or symbols to indicate what you did each day, e.g. "LIFT" or "SH" for self-hypnosis.

Daily Warmup

Track what you do each day for each category, e.g. "JJ" for Jean Jean. Make sure to alternate A and Bb Clarinet each day.

Current workload

Don't neglect current obligations, and track the work you are doing for your school or job.

Excerpts

Track your work on excerpts using symbols and numbers (see key on the left). In Chapter 2, I will describe a strategy for managing this work.

Full Parts Practice

In an audition where excerpts are not specified, I think you should ideally spend time each day either listening to or playing through a section of a full work on your list. You may not be able to learn all the full parts, but if asked, you should be able to sound like you are at least aware of the music. First, listen while looking at your part and noting exposed clarinet moments. Once you've done that, familiarize yourself with those exposed moments by playing them through a few times. Each day, try to listen to or practice something in the music that isn't on your list of excerpts. Note that work here (e.g. "L Shost 1 IV" would mean you listened to the 4th movement of Shostakovich Symphony No. 1).

CHAPTER 2

PRACTICE

Now that you have your materials and a plan, it's time to execute the plan, day by day.

Suggested time: 3–8 weeks

Here, you will find suggestions for how to organize the time you have into four phases: "Get Familiar", "Get to Work", "Get Performing", and "Get Inspired". It might be helpful to map out your schedule and to only read through the sections of this book that match your current phase. Periodically reviewing the suggestions for your current phase will keep you motivated and might give you new ideas as you are working. New things will jump out as helpful or become less useful as you progress through your preparation.

You do not rise to the level
of your goals.
You fall to the level of
your systems.

JAMES CLEAR

Phase 1: Get Familiar
0–2 Weeks

Goals: Become familiar with new repertoire, listen daily to all of the excerpts, and begin slow work on the most difficult technical excerpts.

- Daily warmups
- Physical exercise: 20–30 min
- 5–6 hours of actual playing: 2 or 3 sessions of practice, each 1–2 hours
- 1–2 hours of listening and study with listening list

Skip this Phase if: (1) You are familiar with *all of* the repertoire; or (2) You are not familiar with *any* of the repertoire, since in this case you need to practice everything equally. If case (2) applies to you, spend more time listening to your listening list during *Phase 2*.

Learn unfamiliar repertoire early on to let it "season" throughout the process. Listen to a few recordings of each new piece to get an idea of the variety of tempi or styles you might encounter. You might find it best to concentrate on one work at a time or to spend a bit each day on each new work.

Start the familiar, technical excerpts slowly and give yourself a lot of time to move the tempo up gradually, with the goal of being at performance tempo by two weeks before the audition. Consider starting half-speed, even for familiar excerpts. The comfort this kind of work provides on audition day is such a great feeling! Practice technical work WITH DYNAMICS and PHRASING now, even at very slow tempi. This will ensure your future performance will also be musically compelling.

Find time each day (at least once) to listen through your whole listening list.

The chart on the next page shows which repertoire might be technical and unfamiliar at first, and how you might approach using your practice time during *Phase 1*. Notice how many excerpts remain untouched for me during this phase.

Phase 1 Practice Chart

	M	T	W	Th	F	S	Su	M	T	W	Th	F	S	Su
Exercise	BIKE	LIFT		YOGA	BIKE		BIKE	BIKE	LIFT	BIKE	YOGA	BIKE	YOGA	
Meditation	M	SH	M/SH	M/SH	M	M		M/SH		SH	M	SH	M/SH	M
Warmup	A	Bb	A	Bb	A	Bb	A	Bb	A	Bb	A	Bb	A	Bb
Fingers	JJ100	JJ100	B84	B84	K120	K120	JJ100	JJ100	B84	B84	K92	K92	B96	B96
Articulation	142	143	142	143	144	147	152 :-(	148	150	152	154	156	158	160
Intonation	X	X		X	X	X		X			X	X	X	X
Richmond Rep	BRMS	BRMS		BRMS	PERF	PERF		MHLR	MHLR	MHLR	MHLR	PERF	PERF	
Mozart I														
Mozart II														
Copland	LX	X	X	RLX	X	X	X	RL					X	X
Beethoven 4 II														
Beethoven 4 IV	X	X	X	X	X	X	X						X	X
Beethoven 6 I	X	X	X	X	X	X	X						X	X
Beethoven 6 IIA														
Beethoven 6 IIB														
Beethoven 6 III														
Beethoven 8 trio														
Brahms 3 IA														
Brahms 3 IB														
Brahms 3 II														
Galanta I														
Galanta middle	LX	X	PA	RLX	X	X	X	L	PAX	X	LX	PAX	X	X
Galanta end	LX	X	PA	RLX	X	X	X	L	PAX	X	LX	PAX	X	X
Mend Scherzo														
Mend 3 II														
Mend 3 IV	LX	X	P						PAX	X	LX	X	X	X
Rach 2														
Daphnis Noodles	X	60	6				2	74	76	78	80	82	84	
Daphnis Last 2	XX	X	7				2	84	86	88	90	92	94	
Bolero														
Pines														
Capriccio I	90	92	9					:-(	96	96	96	100 :-)	104	104
Capriccio III														
Capriccio IV														
Scheherazade II														
Scheherazade IIIa														
Scheherazade IIIb														
Scheherazade IIIc														
Scheherazade IIId														
Scheherazade IV														
Schubert 8														
Shost 1 Ia	L	X	X	X	X	X	X	LX	PAX	X	RLX	X	X	X
Shost 1 Ib	L	X	X	X	X	X	X	LX	PAX	X	RLX	X	X	X
Shost 1 Ic	L	X	X	X	X	X	X	LX	PAX	X	RLX	X	X	X
Shost 1 Id	L	X	X	X	X	X	X	LX	PAX	X	RLX	X	X	X
Shost 1 II	LX	X	X	X	X	X	X	LX	PAX	X	RLX	X	X	X
Shost 1 IV all	LX76	X	X	X	X	X	X	LX	X	X	RLX	X	X	X
Shost 9 II														
Shost 9 III	90 :-(	90	90	92	92 :-)	96	96	96	96 :-(	96	96 :-)	98	100	100
Sibelius 1 I														
Sibelius 1 IIIa	L	X	X	X	X	X	X	LX	X	X	X	X	X	X
Sibelius 1 IIIb	L	X	X	X	X	X	X	LX	X	X	X	X	X	X
Don Juan														
Firebird	X	X	X	X	X	X	X	X	X	X	X	X	X	X
Tchaik 6 Ia														
Tchaik 6 Ib														
Tchaik 6 Ic														
Full Parts Practice														

> In an ideal world this work is done daily, but in the real world you will probably miss some days. Just track what you actually do.

> I practice some excerpts in this phase because they are part of my warmup, not because they are unfamiliar or very technical. I still track this practice on my chart.

This is a demonstration of when to practice, not how to practice. These symbols are not an indication of what you should do each day, just an illustration of how to use your chart.

Phase 2: Get to Work
3–6 Weeks

Goals: Divide your list and begin practicing everything methodically. Record yourself and listen back. Play along with recordings to stay musically engaged. Listen to your listening list constantly. Strive to be the most prepared person at the audition! Approach your work with curiosity and creativity!

- Daily warmups
- Physical exercise: 20–30 min
- 5–6 hours of actual playing: 2 or 3 sessions of practice, each 1–2 hours
- 1–2 hours of listening (including full movements) to listening list or recordings of practice
- Get familiar with full parts (10–15 min a day)

It's time to get to work on the list… with a plan. If you already have a plan that works and are just looking for practice ideas, skip to the sections about specifically addressing technical, musical and intonation issues on *page 43*.

Before I take you through my practice plan, it might be worth considering some questions that will guide your practice in this phase.

Should I sit or stand?

If the screen is removed, I stand for the concerto and sit for excerpts. If the entire audition takes place behind a screen, then it's a judgment call. If you can play very soloistically while sitting, your tone might sound better than those standing and pointing their bell at the committee. However, if when you sit you are less musically convincing, you should probably play the concerto standing.

When you can be seen, you look more musically commanding and comfortable as a soloist when you stand. I always prepare to play the concerto standing in case the screen comes down in a final round. For excerpts, I think clarinetists should always sit to play. Whatever you decide, practice that way now.

Should I prepare differently for different orchestras?

When it comes to pitch, YES. If the orchestra in question plays at a specific pitch level, you should be prepared to play at that pitch level, at least for the concerto, because you may be playing with a pianist. Ensemble rounds might be a part of the audition as well. I've also seen committee members looking at tuners while they listen to candidates play.

Pro Tip – Pitch Level

Most orchestras have an official pitch level, which will affect the tuning of the piano for sure. If it isn't indicated on the repertoire list, you can always email to ask. It will usually be 440, 441, or 442. However, with more and more live concerts available online, I suggest playing along with some live recordings just to get a sense of how "honest" they are about holding the pitch.
If an ensemble round happens during or after an orchestra rehearsal, wind players might be slightly higher in pitch. Playing with the live recordings might give you an idea about how "flexible" you should expect to be.

When it comes to style, it can't hurt to have an understanding of the clarinet approach that a particular orchestra has been used to hearing, but you can't really anticipate what they might be looking for now. Additionally, a new music director might take the wind section in a completely new direction with each new hire they make. Do not get carried away trying to be someone you aren't. If you win, you'll spend your career playing in a way you don't necessarily enjoy!

Make the most compelling case for the way YOU play and show them WHY the clarinet should be played this way.

Divide and Conquer

My practice plan begins by dividing the audition excerpts into daily batches. I usually rotate through everything on the list every two days.

Be intentional about dividing up your list. Whatever you do, avoid only practicing technical excerpts because you will get tight, have poor dynamic and expressive control, and neglect the real music of the audition—which is where I believe people win or lose. It's important to practice expressive and slow excerpts early on, if only to remember that making music is beautiful and to remain connected to the human, vocal quality of your sound every day.

Think of a workout routine in a gym. Many people divide up their workouts into specific days (e.g. "leg day" or "shoulders day"). This would be like practicing only technical or expressive excerpts on a particular day of the week. I prefer the "full-body workout" version of practicing every day... a nice balance of each kind of excerpt.

To start creating my rotation, I first divide my list into a few categories:

- **Daily:** Excerpts I need to do every day to feel confident (try to minimize this group)
- **Technical:** Technical excerpts that I can afford to rotate
- **Expressive:** Expressive excerpts
- **Other:** Everything else

On the first day of my rotation I practice all my daily excerpts, along with half of my technical, expressive, and other excerpts. On the second day of my rotation I practice my daily excerpts along with the *other half* of my technical, expressive, and other excerpts.

In my chart, I color-code excerpts according to which day I practice them (see *page 38*). If I practice them daily, I code them yellow; if I practice them on the first day of the rotation, I code them green; and if I practice them on the second day of the rotation, I code them blue. Then I add a matching colored pull tab to each excerpt in my audition book. That way, if I know I am practicing blue on a given day, I can easily work through my book.

This is a bit complicated to describe, but once you set it up it is very simple to use. I have provided some illustrations on the next several pages to help explain a five-step process for how I make these decisions and use my practice chart.

Please note: the following illustrations serve as examples only, I may label Dances of Galanta as "other," but you might label it "technical." These are decisions you need to make for yourself.

1 — Label each excerpt with its category

2 — Group excerpts together by category

	M	T	W	Th	F	S	Su		W	Th	F	S	Su
	A	Bb	A	Bb	A	Bb	A	Bb	A	Bb	A	Bb	A	Bb

Categories (faint, left): Winds / Fingers / Articulation / Intonation / Richmond Rep

Label	Excerpt	Daily (D)	Technical (T)	Expressive (E)	Other (O)
O	Mozart I				Mozart I
E	Mozart II			Mozart II	
T	Copland		Copland		
E	Beethoven 4 II			Beethoven 4 II	
D	Beethoven 4 IV	Beethoven 4 IV			
D	Beethoven 6 I	Beethoven 6 I			
E	Beethoven 6 IIA			Beethoven 6 IIA	
E	Beethoven 6 IIB			Beethoven 6 IIB	
T	Beethoven 6 III		Beethoven 6 III		
O	Beethoven 8 trio				Beethoven 8 trio
O	Brahms 3 IA				Brahms 3 IA
O	Brahms 3 IB				Brahms 3 IB
E	Brahms 3 II			Brahms 3 II	
O	Galanta I				Galanta I
O	Galanta middle				Galanta middle
O	Galanta end				Galanta end
T	Mend Scherzo		Mend Scherzo		
T	Mend 3 II		Mend 3 II		
O	Mend 3 IV				Mend 3 IV
E	Rach 2			Rach 2	
D	Daphnis Noodles	Daphnis Noodles			
T	Daphnis Last 2		Daphnis Last 2		
E	Bolero			Bolero	
E	Pines			Pines	
T	Capriccio I		Capriccio I		
T	Capriccio III		Capriccio III		
O	Capriccio IV				Capriccio IV
O	Scheherazade II				Scheherazade II
T	Scheherazade IIIa		Scheherazade IIIa		
O	Scheherazade IIIb				Scheherazade IIIb
O	Scheherazade IIIc				Scheherazade IIIc
T	Scheherazade IIId		Scheherazade IIId		
T	Scheherazade IV		Scheherazade IV		
E	Schubert 8			Schubert 8	
O	Shost 1 Ia				Shost 1 Ia
O	Shost 1 Ib				Shost 1 Ib
O	Shost 1 Ic				Shost 1 Ic
O	Shost 1 Id				Shost 1 Id
T	Shost 1 II		Shost 1 II		
T	Shost 1 IV all		Shost 1 IV all		
E	Shost 9 II			Shost 9 II	
D	Shost 9 III	Shost 9 III			
E	Sibelius 1 I			Sibelius 1 I	
T	Sibelius 1 IIIa		Sibelius 1 IIIa		
T	Sibelius 1 IIIb		Sibelius 1 IIIb		
E	Don Juan			Don Juan	
D	Firebird	Firebird			
O	Tchaik 6 Ia				Tchaik 6 Ia
E	Tchaik 6 Ib			Tchaik 6 Ib	
E	Tchaik 6 Ic			Tchaik 6 Ic	

Full Parts Practice

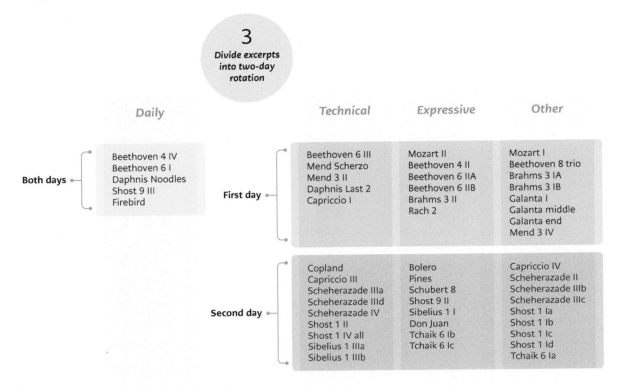

3
Divide excerpts into two-day rotation

Daily | **Technical** | **Expressive** | **Other**

Both days
Beethoven 4 IV
Beethoven 6 I
Daphnis Noodles
Shost 9 III
Firebird

First day

Technical:
Beethoven 6 III
Mend Scherzo
Mend 3 II
Daphnis Last 2
Capriccio I

Expressive:
Mozart II
Beethoven 4 II
Beethoven 6 IIA
Beethoven 6 IIB
Brahms 3 II
Rach 2

Other:
Mozart I
Beethoven 8 trio
Brahms 3 IA
Brahms 3 IB
Galanta I
Galanta middle
Galanta end
Mend 3 IV

Second day

Technical:
Copland
Capriccio III
Scheherazade IIIa
Scheherazade IIId
Scheherazade IV
Shost 1 II
Shost 1 IV all
Sibelius 1 IIIa
Sibelius 1 IIIb

Expressive:
Bolero
Pines
Schubert 8
Shost 9 II
Sibelius 1 I
Don Juan
Tchaik 6 Ib
Tchaik 6 Ic

Other:
Capriccio IV
Scheherazade II
Scheherazade IIIb
Scheherazade IIIc
Shost 1 Ia
Shost 1 Ib
Shost 1 Ic
Shost 1 Id
Tchaik 6 Ia

After writing a letter next to each excerpt on your chart, create a list of the excerpts in each category in order to divide them into two relatively equal practice days.

Ideally, these two days take a similar amount of time to practice as well. You'll see above that I decided to move the Copland Concerto into my blue day in an effort to even-out the work time by splitting up the two solo works (Mozart on the green day, Copland on blue). Once you start practicing using the rotation, you may need to swap excerpts from one group to another. Only swap "like" excerpts and always try to keep the same number of each kind of excerpt on each day. For example, never swap a technical excerpt for an expressive one.

Again, this is only an example of how you might categorize your excerpts. You should make your own decisions.

On the right, you can see how the colors are then added to the practice chart for *Phase 2.* Consider this a depiction of how your chart *might* look after two weeks of practicing this way (in an ideal world). The symbols I use were discussed on *page 28.* This is not a suggestion for *how* to practice, but rather an illustration to show the pattern of *when* you will practice each excerpt. Perhaps the chart looks a little bit empty to you, but trust me, this chart indicates PLENTY of work in the practice room!

Phase 2 Practice Chart

	M	T	W	Th	F	S	Su	M	T	W	Th	F	S	Su
Exercise	BIKE	LIFT	BIKE	YOGA	BIKE				BIKE	LIFT	BIKE		BIKE	YOGA
Meditation	M	SH	M/SH	M/SH		M	M	M/SH			M	SH	M/SH	M
Warmup	A	Bb	A	Bb	A	Bb	A	Bb	A	Bb	A	Bb	A	Bb
Fingers	JJ100	JJ100	B84	B84	K120	K120	JJ100	JJ100	B84	B84	K92	K92	B96	B96
Articulation	142	143 :-(	142 :-)	143 :-)	144	147	152 :-(	148 :-)	150	152	154	156	158	160
Intonation	X	X		X	X	X		X			X	X	X	X
Richmond Rep	MZRT	BTHVN		MZRT	PERF	PERF			STRAV		STRAV	PERF	PERF	
Mozart I			X	RX		LX			PAX		X		X	
Mozart II	X		X	RX		LX			PAX		X		X	
Copland		X		RX		LX		X		PAX		X		X
Beethoven 4 II	X		X	RX		LX			PAX		X		X	
Beethoven 4 IV	112	114	120	R122	R126	L126	LX :-(	126	132	134	136	138	140 :-(	140 :-)
Beethoven 6 I	X	X	X	RX	RX	LX	LX	X	PAX	PAX	X	X	X	X
Beethoven 6 IIA	X		X	RX		LX			PAX		X		X	
Beethoven 6 IIB	X		X	RX		LX			PAX		X		X	
Beethoven 6 III	X		X	RX		LX			PAX		X		X	
Beethoven 8 trio	X		X	RX		LX			PAX		X		X	
Brahms 3 IA	X		X	RX		LX			PAX		X		X	
Brahms 3 IB	X		X	RX		LX			PAX		X		X	
Brahms 3 II	X		X	RX		LX			PAX		X		X	
Galanta I	RLX		X	RX		LX			PAX		RLX		RLX	
Galanta middle	X		X	RX		LX			PAX		X		X	
Galanta end	X		X	RX		LX			PAX		X		X	
Mend Scherzo	X		X	RX		LX			PAX		X		X	
Mend 3 II	X		X	RX		LX			PAX		X		X	
Mend 3 IV	X		X	RX		LX			PAX		X		X	
Rach 2		X		RX		LX		X		PAX		X		X
Daphnis Noodles	X	X	X	RX	RX	LX	LX	X	PAX	PAX	X	X	X	X
Daphnis Last 2	X		XX	RX		LX			PAX		X		XX	
Bolero		X		RX		LX		X		PAX		X		X
Pines		X		RX		LX		X		PAX		X		X
Capriccio I	X		X	RX		LX			PAX		X		X	
Capriccio III		X		RX		LX		X		PAX		X		X
Capriccio IV		X		RX		LX		X		PAX		X		X
Scheherazade II		X		RX		LX		X		PAX		X		X
Scheherazade IIIa		X		RX		LX		X		PAX		X		X
Scheherazade IIIb		X		RX		LX		X		PAX		X		X
Scheherazade IIIc		X		RX		LX		X		PAX		X		X
Scheherazade IIId		X		RX		LX		X		PAX		X		X
Scheherazade IV		X		RX		LX		X		PAX		X		X
Schubert 8		X		RX		LX		X		PAX		X		X
Shost 1 Ia		X		RX		LX		X		PAX		X		X
Shost 1 Ib		X		RX		LX		X		PAX		X		X
Shost 1 Ic		X		RX		LX		X		PAX		X		X
Shost 1 Id		X		RX		LX		X		PAX		X		X
Shost 1 II		X		RX		LX		X		PAX		X		X
Shost 1 IV all		XX		RX		LX		XX		PAX		X		XX
Shost 9 II	X		RLX		RX		LX		PAX					
Shost 9 III	X	X	X	RX	RX	LX	LX	X	PAX	PAX				X
Sibelius 1 I		X		RX		LX		X		PAX				X
Sibelius 1 IIIa		X		RX		LX		X		PAX				X
Sibelius 1 IIIb		X		RX		LX		X		PAX				X
Don Juan		X		RX		LX		X		PAX		X		X
Firebird	X	X	X	RX	RX	LX	LX	X	PAX	PAX	X	X	X	X
Tchaik 6 Ia	X		X	RX		LX			PAX		X		X	
Tchaik 6 Ib	X		X	RX		LX			PAX		X		X	
Tchaik 6 Ic	X		X	RX		LX			PAX		X		X	
Full Parts Practice	LS1I	LS1II	LS1III	LDJ	LSCH	LS1BI	LS1BIII	LM3IV	XM3IV			LPINES	XPINES	

4 Color-code your practice chart

This is a demonstration of when to practice, not how to practice. These symbols are not an indication of what you should do each day, just an illustration of how to use your chart.

Adding colored pull tabs to your audition book is a great way to make your practice routine in *Phase 2* easier to follow. Each tab should have the title of the excerpt written on it. I like to place the tab on the page just *before* the excerpt it matches, so that when I pull the tab, I am immediately taken to the correct excerpt. Although the color coding may only seem to be helpful in *Phase 2*, the pull tabs will remain very useful as you move into later phases and at the audition as well. Being able to access the excerpts quickly and accurately will make it easier to stay calm under pressure.

I don't typically use a pull tab for each excerpt in my book. Sometimes I use a tab for every movement, and sometimes a tab for every symphonic work. Many times all of the excerpts within a movement are the same color, so it's easier to just have a tab for the movement. However, if for whatever reason one of the excerpts is a different color, you need to create a tab for it.

Whether or not you adopt my color coordination method, you should put some pull tabs in your book for quick access. This is one of my favorite ways to make my life easier when practicing and performing. It takes very little time and has a big impact on your efficiency and comfort.

How to use your practice time in Phase 2

Remember, you will be slowly refining this list over the course of weeks or months. You don't have to perfect anything in one sitting, so it's best to set simple, manageable goals for each practice session. Pick one thing you can spend some time improving today, and then move on. Always evaluate your playing for good rhythm, pulse, and intonation (the easiest to forget to fix). Specific recommendations about each are at the end of this section. I like having themed days: play along days, intonation days, mixed up rhythm days, etc. It keeps things fresh. Spend a little time each day playing or listening to some of the full parts on your list just to be familiar with them (10–15 min).

Develop your approach to each excerpt

The following three things should be crystal clear in your mind about each excerpt and rehearsed each time you practice it.

- Decide from where in the music you will get the tempo.
- Think of a one- or two-word, vivid character/physical cue/technical cue to help you get the character right away. Write it at the top of the page!
- In your mind, sing the intro in tempo and with your vivid character. You should be listening to your listening list regularly, and this mental intro should match the intro you used when editing your sound files.

This needs to become habitual: 1–Tempo. 2–Character. 3–Sing the intro in your mind. 4–GO!

Record yourself early and often

Recording yourself will give you a shortcut to the real issues that need to be addressed.

First, invest in a set of nice (over the ear) headphones. Personal recording devices already compress the sound a bit, and listening through phone or laptop speakers or earbuds will further distort the sound. I like using external microphones, because I can set up a mic stand 10–12 ft away and 6–8 ft in the air to give myself some space when I record.

Here are some ways I use a recorder in everyday practice:

- Record one excerpt, then listen right away. Choose one thing to fix and give it 5–7 minutes of practice. Move on. Do I use a timer? Yes!
- Record 4–5 randomized excerpts in a row. Choose one thing to fix in each, give each 5–7 minutes of work. Move on.
- Warm up and record half of the list. Then, set that recording aside for the following day. Once you have started this process, listen to the recording from the day before, and then focus your practice on those excepts. Each day, record half of the list (e.g. green), set it aside, listen to the other half (e.g. blue, from the previous day's recording), and practice based on that recording (e.g. blue). This can help you listen with more objective ears. Take notes as you listen.
- Listen to the recording of the excerpt in your listening list and immediately record your version of it. Listen back to see how yours might be different. I love this one!
- TRY TO BE OBJECTIVE WHEN LISTENING BACK, as though you don't already know your weaknesses. Pick one thing to improve, work on it, then move on.

Divide your practice session using a timer

Using a timer will accomplish two things at once: (1) It keeps you from getting bogged down on the "hard" excerpts; and (2) it forces you to focus on perfecting the "easy" ones. I usually set my timer for 4–6 minutes, and when it goes off I move on. Of course there are some excerpts that take longer just to play—I'm lookin' at you, Daphnis—but even for the longer ones decide ahead of time how much time you'll spend and set a timer. Otherwise you might wear yourself out every day playing the last two pages of Daphnis for three hours.

Plan to move tempo up gradually

Don't go too fast too soon. I start at half tempo in the first week and only add 1 or 2 bpm (beats per minute) each day. If I know the tempo needs to be 140, I start at 70, and I know how many days I'm allowing myself to get to the goal tempo. I plan out exactly how fast I will need to go by the end of each week. Typically, I make sure I am ready to play at the performance tempo by two weeks before the audition.

Play along

Choose a day or two each week to play along with your listening list. It's fun and makes you feel like a musician again. It's also great training for an orchestral excerpt final round of an audition.

Use apps like *SmartMusic*, recordings like *Music Minus One*, or your favorite commercial recording for practicing your concerto. The first two options will help you maintain good pitch and rhythm, and the third option will keep you thinking musically. Better yet, rehearse with a real accompanist! Think of it as preparing for a recital. Remember to practice standing if you intend to stand at the audition.

Use an app like *The Amazing Slowdowner* or *Transcribe+*, which allow you to adjust a recording's speed or pitch to allow you to play along, even if you can't play them up to tempo yet. It might make practicing something like Firebird more fun to play with the music at a slower tempo! You might also use these apps to lower the pitch of a European recording in order to play along.

Create your own practice tracks

I've created arrangements of some of the standard excerpts required at auditions, and they are available in my book called, *Little Scores for Audition Success*. I attribute much of my success to using these arrangements in my preparation. They help me to internalize the music in a way I've never experienced doing anything else.

Pro Tip – Play Along

I believe you should create a play-along track for certain excerpts and keep them on your phone for the warmup room, but there is great value in creating the practice tracks anew each time you prepare. I've found the indelible musical effect is much stronger when I CREATE the track and then use it, rather than simply playing along with a track I created a long time ago. You want to recreate that feeling you have after rehearsing a piece of music in an ensemble for weeks and then waking up each morning hearing it clearly in your head and feeling it in your body.

When you find yourself stuck — technical, musical, and intonation suggestions

Extensive preparation can be overwhelming, and sometimes you need to simplify to keep moving forward. Ask yourself: "What is one thing I can do today to make it better tomorrow?" Do that, and then move on. Here are some ways to change up your approach to technical, musical and intonation issues if you feel stuck. I've also included a one-page summary called "Practice Suggestions" in *Quick Guides* that might be easy to print out and have handy in the practice room for those moments when you need ideas or feel frustrated.

Technical Or Rhythm Issues

Try some of these practice methods in conjunction with your metronome when you get bored, or if you are just looking for new methods that might be more effective for you.

Linking: Start at the last measure and play to the end. When you can play it comfortably ten times without a mistake, add the measure before it and play to the end, when you can play that comfortably ten times without a mistake, add the measure before that. Keep moving backwards. If the passage is too long to play to the end every time, simply play a few measures in a row at a time, but keep moving backward.

Penny Game: At first, this game should be done on only a few beats or measures at a time. Once you've learned it well, you can apply this approach to larger phrases or entire excerpts. Start at your slow tempo and do ten repetitions (reps) without messing up. If all ten reps are correct and feel relaxed, then move the tempo up one click and repeat the process. If you make a mistake, start the ten reps over. I use pennies on my stand to keep track of how many correct reps I've done. It helps me concentrate and simulates performance pressure when you get to the ninth and tenth penny. Try twenty pennies for even more pressure! When you tire of this, you can write down the tempo where you left off and pick it up the next day. If it's impossible to do ten reps without mistakes, consider slowing down, focusing on a shorter bit of music, or using another practice technique.

Mixed-up rhythms: There are plenty or resources online detailing how to do this, and I've found it to be my most useful practice technique. It forces your brain to focus on one note in each grouping, while also allowing your fingers to move quickly through the others. It's like practicing slowly and quickly at the same time.

Offsetting the beat: Place the metronome click on subdivisions other than the downbeat. First, try putting the click on the offbeat. You can also try to put the click on the second or fourth 16th note subdivision.

Practice at tempo: Instead of practicing slowly, you could practice at tempo in very short spurts. Then link the very small pieces together. This doesn't work as well for me, but I've known some people who like this approach.

Interleaved practicing: Instead of looping endlessly on each phrase, try doing only two repetitions, then two on another unrelated phrase, then two on a third, unrelated phrase, then come back to the first and repeat. This also works in phrases with melodic fragments. You can take each fragment alone, practice them out of order, then reassemble the phrase.

Relax your hands and arms: My favorite way to relax my hands and arms is Yehuda Gilad's ping pong ball method. If you haven't heard of this, search "Clarinet lessons, Yehuda Gilad, Masterclass no 6, Brahms 1st Sonata." In this short clip, he explains this helpful exercise that makes the clarinet feel lighter in my hands and instantly makes technical passages feel easier and more fluid.

Weaning off the metronome: If you can play an excerpt but don't seem to have a steady pulse when you record it, you may need to wean yourself off the metronome by removing beats. Try only having a click on beat 1 and 3, then on 2 and 4. Then try only having a click on beat 1 of each measure, then only on beat 2, etc.

Internalizing the pulse with a physical cue: Consider using something like the *Peterson Body-Beat Pulse Solo Metronome Plug-in Accessory*, which is a clip that plugs into your phone or metronome and provides a vibration instead of an audible click. This can help to internalize the pulse in things like the second movement of Beethoven 6 or Bolero.

Mixed meter: Record yourself counting out loud through mixed-meter changes and then play the excerpt along with your recording. This is a great shortcut for mixed-meter work.

Listen at half-speed: Using an app like the *Total Energy Tuner*, record yourself and play it back at half-speed to really narrow the focus of your technical practicing to the real problem areas.

New beats: Use an app like *SuperMetronome* to play along with a new style of beat or rhythm. Playing excerpts against Latin beats or techno beats can be fun, but it can also emphasize and correct new inner rhythmic subdivisions.

Expressive Or Musical Issues

I always found it frustrating when a teacher said there was only one way to correctly play something. As a teacher now, I understand why some teachers are so dogmatic, but the truth is there are multiple convincing ways to play music. Finding *your* way might be difficult at first, but with continued study and experience, it becomes easier.

The simplest way to address a lack of expression is to play along with recordings. Practicing excerpts can really drain you of the joy of making music, and so playing along with commercial recordings, your own recordings of *Little Scores for Success*, *SmartMusic*, or *Music Minus One* can remind you that these simple lines you are practicing alone are actually a part of a much larger and more beautiful work.

Once you have clear ideas, record yourself (sometimes in a big space) to ensure you can hear your ideas clearly. The listener's ear must be carried from moment to moment with a clear plan. Subtle ideas are fine, but sometimes subtlety can be lost on committee members who have been listening to 200 people play the same repertoire. Don't get me wrong, subtlety can be *magical*, but if the people you play for in your mock auditions aren't "getting it," you might need to be more dramatic, or more exaggerated, or you might be more convincing if you try something simpler. Experiment and play for people you trust to decide what will work best.

Listen back to your recording and ask yourself::

– Is it a beautiful sound?
– Is it in tune and in time?
– Are my ideas clear?
– Is there enough dynamic contrast?
– Are there any "dead" spots, where the music is not moving in some way?
– Do I have a plan for where each phrase is going?
– Am I capturing a clear character right from the start?
– Can I make this more special in some way?
– Are there any opportunities to take more risk or create a magical moment?

I do not think you should play excerpts the way you would play within an orchestra. Committee members should be able to "hear" the orchestra in their minds when you play, but if you play it like you'd play with 100 people sitting in front of you, your sound will be too loud or pressed, and it will lack nuance. Think of an audition more like a recital of unaccompanied works for clarinet. Always look for opportunities to build contrast by exploring the possibilities of your *soft* playing. This is especially important for people already playing a job. The audition really requires a level of refinement not often required at work, and there are levels of soft playing you must re-discover after working so hard to project on stage with an orchestra.

One of my rules for myself is to never give the impression I've hit a limit. When your sound "plateaus"—in loud or soft dynamics, or when you press your sound and instead of getting big, it spreads or gets harsh—you've communicated a clear limit in your playing. When you play so softly that you can't shape phrases any more or your sound loses it's core, you've hit a limit. Hitting a limit means that any additional musical energy will be wasted and your sound will simply stay the

same or become dysfunctional in some way. You want your musical ideas to translate into clear shapes and colors in the sound.

Here are some specific ideas to explore expression:

Play along: Play along with a great recording.

Search: Search for new recordings that might spark some passion for this excerpt.

Record yourself: Record yourself and listen back for personality and musical conviction. Experiment and push the limits of your expression.

Copy: Copy a favorite recording until it feels like your own. Copy a recording you don't like just to experiment with different expression.

Imitate: Take on the musical personality of someone famous and imitate how they might play it. Then, try someone different. I've always been surprised when I say jokingly, "So-and-So would play it like this!" and after my imitation, my listener responds, "Yes! THAT was convincing!"

Sing: Sing phrases out loud.

Sing 2× fast: Sing or play the phrase twice as fast to see if larger shapes present themselves naturally.

Chamber music: Pretend you are playing in a chamber ensemble and communicate musically to the imaginary musicians with whom you are playing (I love this one).

Intonation Issues

Here are a few ways to work on intonation that I've found helpful:

Drone: Choose a root note to use as a drone (usually the key center). Play the excerpt against the drone. Record it and listen back to be really picky.

Pitch matching: Use a pitch-matching function in an app, such as *Tonal Energy Tuner*, with headphones. It will play the correct pitch in your ear as you play.

Graph: Record yourself with *Tonal Energy Tuner* and observe the resulting graph of your inaccuracies.

Playback through speakers: Record yourself playing the excerpt and play it back through speakers while watching the tuner. Doing this will reveal how you might be hearing (and then playing) intervals incorrectly. It will also reveal "problem" notes that you've been ignoring.

Practice track: Create a practice track with a drone using the scores in the book, *Little Scores for Audition Success*.

Keyboard: Record the excerpt on a keyboard and listen a few times to try and get more accurate intervals in your ear.

Sing: Sing the excerpt with a drone.

Clarinet Pitfalls

Aside from basic tone quality, there are some things I've noticed that committees are very slow to forgive, so I try to avoid these common pitfalls whenever possible. When many people play with the same issues, it becomes hard to listen past them for musicianship.

Pressing your sound: Pushing beyond the limit of your sound or compressing the shape of the tone as you get louder is usually the result of pushing too hard, biting, or having tension in your throat. Remember:

- There's no need to project in this context.
- Build in dynamic contrast on the soft side whenever possible.
- Do not force your sound unless it is for a specific musical effect. If "forcing" is a default way of playing loudly, it will never sound musically intentional, even when it is!
- Focus on resonance instead of trying to play louder.

Air leaks: When you are behind a screen, it's like playing under a microscope and everything is amplified. An air leak can distract the committee from hearing your musical ideas. To address this:

- Work to strengthen your embouchure, especially the corners. Several devices can help (e.g. *The Facial Flex* and the *Wind-O*)
- Play double lip in your practice. Simply roll your top lip over your top teeth the same way you roll your bottom lip, preventing the teeth from contacting the mouthpiece. This will keep you from biting and will strengthen the muscles of the embouchure.
- Sensitizing your ears. Once you realize you are doing it, you might be able to just stop!

False accents in articulation (i.e. "twang"):
Attempts to make a clear start to the note can sometimes create unintended accents. Remember:

- This is the result of biting on the attack or from moving your tongue too much in the approach, release, or both.
- Practice attacks with a tuner to ensure you are not biting. Focus on starting the note in exactly the voicing you want, without pressing your jaw up for security.

Flat throat tones: Be careful to not let the pitch sag, especially when using American-pitched mouthpieces and especially in louder dynamics. To address this issue:

- Be meticulous about checking excerpts that include throat tones. F#, F, E, Eb are all problem notes for me, and I need to find fingerings to improve their resonance and pitch.

Phase 3: Get Performing
1–2 Weeks Before Audition

Goals: Pull numbers out of a hat to create "rounds" to record. Play mock auditions. Polish your first round into immaculate condition.

- Daily warmups
- Physical exercise: 20–30 min
- 5–6 hours of actual playing: 2 or 3 sessions of practice, each 1–2 hours
- 1 hour or less of listening back to practice recordings and or playing along with listening list

It's time to practice performing. That means simulating performance situations as often as you can. Rehearsing your approach to each excerpt (from *Phase 2*) in deliberate ways becomes important here. You need to have a plan for your thoughts, both while you are playing each excerpt, and during the silence between excerpts (this will be addressed below). At this point, I let go of my color-coded rotation system and replace it with practicing the list in randomized groups.

Create "rounds" and practice excerpts in groups

Number your whole list, cut up paper with numbers on it, and pull numbers out of a "hat" for randomizing your performances. Record a group of four to seven at a time, then work on it. Perhaps record it again. Do not return the numbers to the hat until you've gotten through the whole list. When you've done them all, return the numbers, mix them up, and do it again.

Think of each group of excerpts as a mini-recital

Focus on maximizing your expressive and dynamic range. How might you rethink this particular performance, given this specific group of excerpts? Where can you show off how softly you can play? How might you play differently to make similar excerpts sound different from each other if they randomly get pulled out of a hat in succession?

Get EXCITED by silence

Expect and be excited by the silence at the beginning and end of everything you play. It's a blank canvas for you to paint! When doing run-throughs,

hear the silence, get excited, and then make music! At the end of each excerpt, make sure to take extra care with how you exit into silence. Think of yourself tying each excerpt off with a beautiful bow to leave a smile on the audience's face. Rehearse the skill of not thinking about what you've just played once it's over. Whether it went well or not, practice letting it go and focusing on the next amazing excerpt to perform! Create a ritual of finishing an excerpt with care, and moving on intentionally to the next.

Polish your first-round repertoire

As your audition approaches, *polish the first-round repertoire into immaculate condition!* The first-round excerpts will likely include: Mozart Concerto exposition, Beethoven 6 (Movements 1 and 2), Brahms 3 (Movements 1 and 2), and Mendelssohn Scherzo. There are going to be auditions where the first round is different than these, but in my experience these are included in the first round of most auditions. Maybe you think you know these well, but spend some time making them GREAT! It won't matter how much you practiced the obscure Eb clarinet tutti passages in the middle of the Shostakovich symphony if you don't impress them with your Brahms 3 or Beethoven 6.

Schedule a few mock auditions and commit to dates and times with people

I'd suggest at least three mock auditions during this phase. Give yourself a few days in between to process the experience and recalibrate for the next.

Mock auditions are opportunities to rehearse your planned performance in front of an audience. This is a different experience than the practice room, and these mocks are opportunities to visualize your actual audition. Your anxiety will be higher, so you can practice how to handle distractions that come along. If you are considering the use of beta blockers, use these to test your timing and dosage (See "Information About Beta Blockers" in *Quick Guides*). Having the extra audition book can make it easier for a listener to give you helpful feedback (see "Make your audition book" on *page 18*).

Try doing each mock audition in a different acoustic environment: big churches, dead gymnasiums, rehearsal rooms, stages, etc. You want to get some experience dealing with the distractions of an unknown sonic space. Record each from a distance, and listen back later.

The more you can use these opportunities to visualize the actual audition, the more beneficial they will be. Practice walking to your chair in silence with all of your gear. Maybe put up a screen. Have a friend pretend to be the music director and ask you to try things differently on the spot. Do anything you can to simulate the experience.

Find your trusted ears

When playing for other people, it's important to find trusted ears. These are people you admire and trust as musicians and who are able to communicate to you in supportive ways that move you toward your goals.

Feedback needs will look different for different people. Some people crave direct, clear feedback. Others like a gentler, more supportive listener. Some people are inclined to the more artistic side of music-making and need trusted ears for pitch and rhythm. Others are detail oriented and need a musical coach to inspire them to be an artist. As the audition gets closer, consider asking people to listen without offering feedback, as you will be cementing your ideas and may not be as open to

making changes. They will still be able to help create a high pressure situation just by being there to hear you.

Play for non-clarinetists! The majority of a committee will be musicians who play other instruments, and they are less likely to forgive the bad habits we all have associated with navigating this instrument. In my experience, clarinetists can be so attached to their own interpretations that may not be as open to yours.

Remember: You will likely never play for someone and have them say, "Yep, that was great! I have no comments!" People will always have opinions and ideas. That doesn't negate your ideas or mean you aren't ready. You shouldn't use mock auditions for validation. They are simply a way to get some feedback, get some new ideas, and practice performing under pressure in front of an audience.

Consider your reeds

Elsewhere in this book, I talked about building dynamic contrast on the soft side, so I opt for a reed that is lighter than what I would normally use in the orchestra. Finding a reed that will accomplish this while giving me a bit of support when I need to make a big sound is tricky. It also requires me to push myself to practice making a bigger sound on more responsive reeds without losing the sound quality I want.

Opposite: Dr. Andrea Vos-Rochefort coaches Meaghan Rodriguez at Texas A&M University-Kingsville. Photo by Vincent Rochefort Photography.

Phase 4: Get Inspired and Ready – Last Few Days

Goals: Record the start of every excerpt each day to ensure the right character from the first note. Visualize having a great time. Find ways to have fun. Taper your practice time. Create audition survival kits. Decide what you will wear for the audition. Get lots of sleep.

- Daily warmups
- Physical exercise: 20–30 min
- 2–3 hours in a day: Ideally, get 2 or 3 sessions of practice, each 1–2 hours
- Listening to inspiring music

Use this time to taper your technical practicing and really turn up your inspiration and joy about music. Focus on making special musical moments really beautiful and that the character of everything you play is apparent from the first note. Keep listening to recordings and reflect on how lucky we are to be musicians!

The work has been done now, and the most important and powerful thing you can do at this point is to relax, rest and get inspired.

What to do

- Visualize the audition performance often. (See "Visualization" on *page 25*)
- Work on technical excerpts but make them fun. Try the *SuperMetronome* app to play with different kinds of beats.
- Record only the beginnings of excerpts to practice ensuring character from the start of each.
- Relax and have some fun. See a movie, take a walk, go to a museum, dance.
- Sleep

The work has been done now, and the most important and powerful thing you can do at this point is to relax, rest and get inspired.

What to pack

Assemble your "Audition Survival Kit".

Remember that you may feel like you are "camping out" at the hall during the audition. Deliberations, delays, security considerations, weather, and other circumstances can contribute to you being stuck without food or water for hours longer than expected. You'll have no control over your environment (e.g. what you see/hear, the temperature, the schedule). See the page on the right for a list of items that I ALWAYS plan to pack for my audition trip.

Acquire a "Stage Kit".

Get a small bag, such as a camera case, to hold everything you will bring to the stage with you. This makes the chaos of getting to and from the stage easier when you are nervous and want to focus on music. In the warm up room, you will fill this kit with a few items (see right), and your trip to the stage will be worry-free, focused, and inspired.

My Audition Survival Kit

☐ **Ear plugs:** For the hotel or warmup room to block out other players.

☐ **Headphones:** For the green room. Even if there's nothing playing, they say, "I'm not interested in gabbing."

☐ **Water:** Very important.

☐ **Hypnosis or meditation:** On your phone.

☐ **Good book:** Something that holds your attention. I've had auditions where they confiscated my phone for the duration of the audition. Be ready with your ear plugs and low-tech ways to pass the time.

☐ **Recording device:** To record the beginnings of excerpts at the hotel or to possibly record your audition round from your pocket or from your "Stage Kit" (you might also just use your phone).

☐ **Inspiring music playlist:** This music must be personal to you and help you feel a sense of BEAUTY, DRAMA, and SENSITIVITY. This is not your excerpt listening list. It will be used in the warmup room to stay inspired about being a musician. I like to listen to my favorite opera moments and amazing chamber music. If you want to be really safe, load it onto a device other than your phone in case phones are confiscated for security purposes.

☐ **Hand warmers:** I always use these in the warmup room. They add to my feeling of confidence and are available at any store that carries outdoor gear.

☐ **Snacks:** You can't have too many. I use Power Bars.

☐ **Cigarette paper:** To quickly deal with water bubbles under a pad.

☐ **Pencil:** To mark alterations to your excerpts if they've made changes or to make notes as you plan your round.

☐ **Reeds in an air-tight container with a Humidipak:** To mitigate climate issues with your reeds. I use Humidipaks from D'Addario and a sandwich container from Target that cost me $1.50.

☐ **Beta Blockers:** If you want them and have a prescription. Please see "Information about Beta Blockers" in *Quick Guides* at the end of this book.

☐ **Travel umbrella:** For your walks to and from the hall.

☐ **Breath builder:** If you don't keep it in your case.

☐ **Photo album on your phone:** To use in the warmup room. It should be full of things that make you laugh or feel extremely grateful.

My Stage Kit

☐ **Pencil:** To mark your own parts if they change measure numbers they want.

☐ **Recording device or phone:** To use if you are planning to record your round.

☐ **Reed case**

☐ **Cigarette paper**

☐ **Swab**

Recording auditions

Many orchestras have policies strictly forbidding recording devices during auditions. However, if they don't, it might be a useful way to get an idea of how you really play under pressure. Do you play things faster than you thought? Was the technical "flub" you thought you made really a big deal? If this is something you want to do, plan on using your phone or a small recording device in your stage kit, or wearing a blazer with a front pocket.

Note: I'd suggest limiting the information you take from a recording like this. You can probably rely on what you hear to evaluate pitch, wrong notes, technical issues, rhythm, and tempo. I wouldn't trust what you hear in regards to your sound or your dynamic range, as these are affected dramatically by the space and proximity of the device.

What to wear

You don't need to wear a suit or a gown, but dress as though you respect the institution for which you are auditioning. If the screen comes down, you want to look professional. You'll see some candidates dressed very casually and some dressed very formally. Many people will wear black concert attire. I either wear all black or dress as I would for a rehearsal with a big orchestra (i.e. slacks, button down, nice shoes).

Don't Forget!

Bring a sweater for layering, even if it's 110 degrees outside. Air conditioning can be brutal in the warmup room!

CHAPTER 3

PERFORM

You've done all the planning and hard work, now it's time to *enjoy* playing for the committee.

Suggested time: Travel days and audition days

This chapter will help you navigate the steps between your home studio and the stage with advice about how to use your time in the hotel and at the audition on audition day.

When you are inspired by
some great purpose,
some extraordinary project,
all of your thoughts break
their bonds. Your mind transcends
limitations; your consciousness
expands in every direction;
and you find yourself in a new,
great and wonderful world.
Dormant forces, faculties and talents
become alive and you discover
yourself to be a greater person than
you ever dreamed yourself to be.

PATANJALI

At the Hotel

Goals: Stay relaxed and rested. Find a way to warm up. Choose the audition reed. Practice for security and confidence (play technical stuff slowly), but don't overdo it. Continue exercise, warmup, and mental training routines.

Check-in

Mention you're taking an important audition and you'll need to make some noise in your room. They may move you to a place where you won't affect other guests or offer the use of a meeting room or a ballroom. Be prepared to pay a small rental fee for the larger spaces. I've never had to pay, but I know others who have.

The day before you play

- Try not to practice for more than 1–2 hours. Remember to practice for security and confidence.
- Do your warmup routine to try and make the experience feel normal.
- Play through technical passages slowly. Rehearse your mental approach to each excerpt, and practice starting the first few measures of each excerpt in the right character from the first note.
- Choose *the* reed for audition day. Don't play too much on it.
- Limit TV time. Read your book, walk around the neighborhood, go for a run, or do a simple workout (if that is part of your normal routine).
- Do visualization or self-hypnosis.
- Review "Audition Protocol" in the *Quick Guides* section of this book.
- Have a nice meal but no alcohol.
- Go to bed early.

Which reed should you use?

There is no such thing as a perfect reed. Reeds that sound amazing in the softest dynamics will sound pretty bad if you try to play your loudest. Likewise, the reeds that hold their sound at the loudest dynamics might render soft playing pale, colorless, and sharp in pitch. I want good response, beautiful color, and expression in the soft dynamics. I also don't want to be walking on egg shells in the louder excerpts, so the reed will need to have some "hold" in it. On a scale of 1–10, from softest to hardest, I'd look for a 4 or a 5, depending on the repertoire.

To simplify, I imagine the audition is an intimate chamber music concert, and I ask myself "Which reed would I be excited to play this chamber concert on?"

The morning of the audition

- Eat something light and protein-rich. Avoid drinking or eating anything hot that would burn your tongue or the roof of your mouth (e.g. continental breakfast coffee, Starbucks microwaved breakfast sandwiches—I've played many auditions with a burned mouth thanks to Starbucks.)
- Warm up on the audition reed.
- Play some technical passages slowly.
- Check touchy spots.
- I try to limit this warmup to 20 minutes. Do not play more than 30–45 min.
- If the reed feels funky, check some others, but try to make this decision in the hotel, rather than the audition warmup room. I sometimes end up playing my backup reed because I'm more comfortable on it since I've been trying to save the "good" one!
- Do visualization or self-hypnosis.
- Pack up your "Audition Survival Kit" and "Stage Kit" for the day (see *page 51*).
- Plan to walk from the hotel to arrive at check-in time or one hour before you are scheduled to play.
- Possibly take your beta blocker now (see "Information About Beta Blockers" in *Quick Guides*).

At the Audition

Goals: Be friendly but stay focused, even between rounds. Manage anxiety with an array of activities to keep you busy.

Check-in and holding room.

Check in with the audition coordinator. You may be drawing numbers. If you draw a later number and will have to wait more than two hours to play, consider heading back to the hotel. The walk will do you some good, and you'll avoid the mind games that will crop up sitting in a room full of nervous people.

There will likely be a green room or a holding room for candidates who are waiting for individual warmup rooms.

- Say hello to friends briefly.
- Find a spot for yourself. Put on headphones and get out your book.
- Do not use a group warmup room. They will likely offer you a private room twenty minutes to an hour before you'll play.
- Be nice to everyone but keep chit-chat to a minimum. You'll have time to catch up later. Politely tell them, "I'm just going to stay in the zone for now." They'll get it.
- If you choose to take beta blockers and didn't take them before arriving, make your way to the bathroom to take them (see "Information About Beta Blockers" in *Quick Guides*).

Warmup room

This is how I use my time in the warmup room. Think of this list as a countdown to the time of your audition.

60 minutes before your audition time

- Turn your phone on airplane mode. You don't want disruptions.
- Open hand warmers and keep them in your hands when not playing.
- Put in your earplugs when not listening to music to block out clarinet players near you.
- Stretch or do yoga. Try a Superman pose (hands on hips, chest out, upright and confident) with earplugs in.
- Read "Direction of Intention" over and over. (*Quick Guides*)
- If they've given you the repertoire for the round, write out the key character words for each excerpt you'll be covering over the round so you can see the variety of expression you'll be presenting. I take a blank sheet of paper and write them from top to bottom on the left side of the page, then leave it sticking out from behind my audition book as I play to serve as a visual reminder of the emotional journey I would like the committee to take with me.
- Review the list of excerpts in this round and carefully check measure numbers against your audition book. Make any necessary corrections with your pencil in your book.
- Listen to inspiring music list (see "Audition Survival Kit" in on *page 51*) and remember how lucky you are to be a musician.

- Remind yourself that you will have the opportunity to inspire the audience (committee) in the same way.
- Review "Audition Protocol" in the *Quick Guides* at the end of this book if you are new to the experience.
- Hydrate.
- Smile—this can trigger real happiness and confidence!

40 minutes before your audition time

- Twenty-minute guided self-hypnosis.
- Hydrate.
- Smile.

20 minutes before your audition time

- Play a few scales to check your reed. Only consider changing your reed if something fundamental won't work. Try the high G in Beethoven 8 or short articulations in Brahms 3 first movement, etc. You may not like the sound of the reed in this room, but trust your selection in the hotel or at home instead of stressing about it now.
- Play along with practice tracks on your phone that you created with *Little Scores for Audition Success* (if you created them in Phase 2).
- Review your list of character words for the round and practice starting excerpts in the right character.

- Use your breath builder to keep your air relaxed.
- Reread "Direction of Intention".
- Look at photos that make you laugh or smile.
- Assemble your "Stage Kit" (Phase 4)— are you going to record your audition? This would be the time to put your device in your "Stage Kit" along with the following: pencil, reed case, cigarette paper, and swab.
- Do a Superman pose: stand up straight, shoulders back, and pretend you are superman for a few minutes.
- If the audition is running behind, keep doing these last few steps, and do not play too much. Stay flexible, inspired, happy, and hydrated. Read a book and keep your mind occupied. I like listening to the introduction to the first movement of the concerto in order to feel like I'm getting ready to perform something really beautiful.
- Swab constantly.
- Remember, everyone is facing the same challenges. If the reeds feel harder on audition day, they will for everyone. If the hall sounds terrible to you, it will to everyone. Respond with grace and poise.

5–10 minutes before your audition time

- Press "record" on your device if you are recording your round.
- Continue the above activities until you are called to play!

After You Play

- Pretend you will have to play again: No chit-chatting about how it went. If your friends ask how it went, simply reply, "I think it went well. We'll see what happens!"
- Don't ask how other people did.
- Stay focused.

If you have to play again the same day

- If you have time, go back to the hotel.
- Some orchestras will not allow you to leave and may even confiscate your phone for the duration of the audition round, even if you have been cut! Be prepared with low-tech ways to keep your mind occupied (e.g. a good book, puzzles, Rubik's Cube).
- Avoid hanging out with other people. This isn't time to socialize. It's time to stay relaxed, happy, and inspired.
- Do something to unwind and take your mind off of the audition for a bit.
- Have some food.
- Go for a walk.
- Do visualization, self-hypnosis, or meditation.
- DO NOT practice Daphnis and Peter and The Wolf for hours. Trust yourself and realize they already love what you are doing. If you need to do some playing at the hotel to feel your best, just keep it to a minimum and remember to focus on building relaxation, joy, and confidence. However, I'd suggest not playing until you get in the warmup room again. You've got this!

If you have to return to play the next day

- Walk back to the hotel.
- Avoid hanging out with other clarinetists too much (or at all).
- Do something to unwind and take your mind off the audition for a bit.
- Exercise
- Go for a walk, read, or visit a museum (if you need to kill more time).
- Call someone you love.
- Play a bit that evening if you want.
- Do visualization, self-hypnosis, or meditation.
- Have good meal (no alcohol).
- Go to bed early.

What if you WIN?

Terrific! Congrats!

You might be introduced to members of the committee and the Music Director. Be ready to make a first impression that is friendly, relaxed, and comfortable.

Most likely, you will not be asked to sign anything that day. They will be in touch in the following days, weeks, and months about employment. In the following chapter, I will offer some thoughts about feedback and contract negotiation.

CHAPTER 4

PROCESS

Whether you win, advance, or lose, there are lessons to be learned.

Suggested time: A week or two after the audition

Here, you will find information about processing your experience, getting feedback, and making use of the feedback in a helpful way. I've also included some thoughts about negotiating a contract so that when your day comes, you'll know what to expect.

It takes humility to seek
feedback. It takes wisdom to
understand it, analyze it
and appropriately act on it.

STEPHEN COVEY

After the Audition

No matter the outcome, there are lessons to be learned. Sometimes you will need to draw your own conclusions and give yourself some feedback about your preparation or the way you handled the challenges of the audition day, and sometimes you will be able to get valuable feedback from those who heard your audition.

Elimination in the first round

Elimination is the most common outcome of an audition. In some ways, I think it is harder to get through the first round than any other round of an audition. The sheer number of candidates playing the same repertoire for days on end creates a real challenge for the committee to listen with their best ears to every player. In Round One there may be an imaginary benchmark of quality, rather than players being compared to each other.

It's hard to learn from an audition when you feel like you did everything you were supposed to do, yet were cut after a few excerpts. You might have been eliminated for a simple reason, like you didn't have the right sound, or you unknowingly played out of tune or out of rhythm. Maybe it was something out of your control, like the committee was very hungry and grumpy and none of the candidates were getting enough votes to advance. Maybe you played in a round with several very strong players and the committee was nervous about advancing so many from the same round.

If you get cut in the first round, try and give yourself some feedback about your preparation and about how you handled the day. Were you extremely nervous? If so, can you figure out why? How will that change the way you prepare in the future? Take notes on the worksheets included in *Quick Guides*.

For example: I remember checking in at auditions, glancing at the sign-in sheet, and seeing names of people who intimidated me. Then, I'd make my way to the green room, where I'd see those musicians sitting around waiting to play. My negative self-talk would start: "What are YOU doing here? These people are REAL musicians, and they always win everything. You are a phony. You don't really have a chance!" Then, when it was my turn to play, I could hear whispers of the committee members behind the screen and pencils on paper. I KNEW what they were writing: "Wow, not good. Out of tune. Terrible sound."

I didn't need any comments from the committee to tell me why I didn't advance. It was as though I had convinced myself that I was not going to advance before the committee even heard me! I knew I needed to address this negative spiral, so I went home and created my "sign-in sheet from hell." I got a clipboard and wrote down all of the names of the people I could think of who might trigger this reaction for me. It was a surprisingly long list! I put the list at the entrance to my practice room and practiced seeing it. Then, I loaded photos of each of the intimidating people onto an electric picture frame on my desk and had it rotate through the pictures constantly. I also changed my self-talk and I rehearsed this new mental script each time I entered the practice room. I reminded myself regularly that these were all people just like me, who made mistakes and felt pressure just like I did. I've worked really hard to be able to play at their level. In addition to humanizing the other musicians, there was no reason to be scared because, behind a screen, the audition process was completely anonymous. I practiced seeing them, wishing them luck, and then focusing on my performance only.

Then, I recorded myself writing with a pencil on paper, whispering, and audibly turning pages in a notebook. I looped that sound in a sound-editing program and played it through my speakers during my mock auditions to practice my reaction to hearing those sounds under pressure. Now, I could choose to hear the sound of writing on paper and picture the words saying things like, "Wow, THAT WAS BEAUTIFUL. This person is a true ARTIST. We've got to hire him!" As I heard pages turn, I imagined the committee looking at each other, smiling and having just written, "No need to hear more... he's our man!" This proved to be a powerful practice. It transformed something that had given me so much anxiety in the past into something that made me feel more confident!

Learning doesn't have to be so dramatic. It can just be a few practical lessons learned. My "Audition Survival Kit" (mentioned in Phase 4) is the result of many less-than-ideal experiences: freezing cold warmup rooms, auditions running hours behind, ending up in a hotel with someone playing Daphnis ALL NIGHT LONG next to me. Take your experiences, write them down, and plan creatively for the next time.

Elimination in the Semi-Finals or Finals

You may have advanced past the preliminaries and been cut in later rounds. This is great! Such a result should boost your confidence and give you fuel to keep going! It can be hard to know at this stage if you were eliminated because of a lack of perfection or because you weren't musically convincing. In the semi-finals and beyond, committee members might have taken more detailed notes as they have begun comparing candidates to each-other. It might be helpful to seek feedback from them in some way.

Getting feedback

Sadly, feedback can difficult to get in this business. Some orchestras have a policy of "no feedback," and others have an existing mechanism to receive feedback easily. If you or your teacher knows someone in the wind section, it might be worth an email or phone call to see if they might offer any advice going forward.

The only caveat I can offer is that people very often only write down bad things. With that in mind, the feedback might not offer encouragement. It's still very valuable, but don't expect to be told how well you played. The notes they take just aren't that detailed. Also, if you get feedback from more than one person on the committee, it might conflict. Look for areas of overlap. This is also true from audition to audition. If one person says your pitch is bad, but usually intonation is not a problem for you, don't freak out. If you hear it twice or more... fix it!

Processing feedback in a helpful way

Perhaps you were proud of some aspect of your performance and insecure about another. You may feel fairly confident you know why you didn't advance. Then you found a way to get feedback, and the feedback came as a complete surprise. How can you process this in a helpful way?

Rule #1: Don't over-correct or give yourself "issues".

If you get comments about your rhythm, check it and pay attention to it, but don't assume you have terrible rhythm.

If you get comments about pitch, try some new ideas mentioned in this book to pay attention to it, but don't become insecure about your ears. Many times, pitch comments are more subjective than you might expect.

If you get comments about your sound, ask yourself if you were pressing your sound beyond its limit and it could have been more refined. Perhaps your sound was diffuse and too stuffy for what they wanted. Sound is the most subjective quality in your playing, and there will be wind sections where your sound just isn't the right fit.

In general, do not make any substantial changes to your approach or your equipment until you get consistent feedback from various sources that there is a problem that needs to be addressed.

Rule #2: Realize your perception might be less accurate than you think.

It is possible that your insecurity about one aspect of your playing and overconfidence about another aspect of your playing led you to prepare in such a way that your weaknesses and strengths swapped! Maybe you were so worried about technique that you put all of your effort into perfecting it, and now it sounds great despite your worry. In contrast, maybe you forgot to check your intonation because people have always told you how great your pitch is. Now it's a problem because you didn't pay much attention to it.

Sometimes the hall itself can alter your perception. Maybe you felt a technical fumble (that may not have been audible in the hall), and you become so distracted by this "flub" that you lost musical intention and your phrasing suffered. You left thinking it was a technical glitch that kept you from advancing, but the committee might have just been bored by your distracted playing. This is important! Without knowing the truth, you'd hunker down and try to be even more perfect the next time, when in reality, you'd benefit more from mental training to let small mistakes go while performing.

Rule #3: Don't freak out.

Any feedback is one person's perception of your performance and is heavily influenced by many factors that are not in your control. Remember, there may have been others on the committee who felt differently about your playing.

Contracts

My sincere hope is that each of you finds a place in this musical world to do what you love and get paid for it. Should you find yourself the winner of an orchestral audition, it helps to know what to expect.

Note: this advice applies to auditions in The United States. Europe and Asia might be different.

If you were auditioning for a titled (not "section") position, you may be able to negotiate your contract before you sign it. Overscale is the first detail of a contract like this that needs to be addressed. Of course there are exceptions, but in general, the bulk of the positions in an orchestra are paid a base scale. Musicians holding titled ("Principal", "Solo", "Assistant-Principal", etc.) positions can sometimes negotiate to be paid an additional percentage of that base scale because of the exposed, soloistic nature of the position they will be filling. This percentage is called "overscale". In some orchestras, there is a set overscale for positions. In others, there is some flexibility.

Some things you might be able to negotiate other than your overscale percentage include moving expenses or additional paid time off. There are attorneys and other professional negotiators who can help you, or you might decide to negotiate for yourself. I've done it both ways and have had mostly positive experiences. There are pros and cons to both approaches.

Negotiating for yourself

Pros

- Negotiating for yourself will be less expensive up front because you won't be paying a lawyer.
- Some people prefer to speak for themselves and feel negotiators can be unnecessarily aggressive.
- You will get a sense of your future management right away.
- You can respond in creative ways specific to you.

Cons

- Unless you ask colleagues about their contracts, which is awkward and sometimes unwelcome, you don't really have a frame of reference for what you might be able to expect.
- You might feel uncomfortable pushing for what you feel you are worth, or you might not fully know what you are worth, and end up undervaluing yourself.
- You might lack experience in negotiating and agree to terms that are less favorable because of information you haven't learned yet.

Hiring a negotiator

Pros

- Negotiators handle all conversations with management for you.
- They might represent multiple clients in your orchestra and in others, which provides them with insider knowledge of the contracts your colleagues might have or the contracts other orchestras are offering.
- They might contact your colleagues in your new orchestra to ask on your behalf about contract issues. These conversations would be very awkward for you to have if you've not yet met your colleagues.

Cons

- Fees can be charged as a flat rate or by the hour but may end up being several thousand dollars to negotiate a contract. In the end, you might not see enough advantage using their services to justify paying that kind of money.
- The communication is a triangle between you, the management and your negotiator. Some things can get lost in the confusion that might result.
- Management might take a more aggressive stance in a negotiation with a seasoned negotiator, and initial offers might be lower and more restrictive than they would be if the management was dealing with you alone.

You will need to advocate for yourself, whether you use a negotiator or not, by doing your own research and having in mind what you want. I advise reaching out and asking around about what is a common practice in terms of negotiations among those musicians who fill a similar role to you in the orchestra. If you are non-confrontational or accommodating

by nature, you may want a negotiator. When going this route, you will likely be charged by the hour (or the minute) by a negotiator, so consider doing the majority of your communications by email. It saves time (and money) and leaves a paper trail of discussions that can be very useful. You might also be able to negotiate a flat fee for their service rather than paying an hourly rate. If there is little chance of having any leverage because of the nature of the position being filled or because of the nature of the orchestra, then I see no need to pay someone to negotiate for you.

Try to remember, in most instances, orchestra managers are not going to try to take advantage of you. Very few orchestras and very few positions within those orchestras have the kind of leeway built into them that would require difficult negoti-

ation. In most cases, there is a very narrow window of flexibility with regards to the terms of your employment, and it's in the interest of both parties that you are happy with your contract and stay a member of the orchestra for a long time.

The audition screen in Orchestra Hall (Detroit, Michigan), home of the Detroit Symphony Orchestra.
Photo by Assistant Principal Bassoonist Michael Ke Ma.

Final Thoughts

Auditioning is a necessary part of your life as a musician. It can be easy to feel overwhelmed by the amount of music to learn or frustrated by just how inhuman the process might seem, but I encourage you to accept the things you cannot change about the process and embrace the challenges you encounter as you would while solving a puzzle or playing a game. Become a student of the audition process. Stay as inspired as an artist, and as competitive as an athlete! I truly believe that approaching your preparation in an organized, consistent and creative way will ensure that you continue to learn from your experiences, improve your performance under pressure, and develop skills and mental toughness that will serve you well, long after your audition days are over.

Quick Guides

Information About Beta Blockers

The information here is not intended, nor implied to be, a substitute for professional medical advice. It is provided for educational purposes only. *Always seek the advice of your physician or other qualified healthcare provider before starting any new treatment or medication.*

For years, doctors have been prescribing beta blockers as an off-brand (used to treat something they were not intended to treat) treatment for performance anxiety related to a variety of situations. Beta blockers affect the heart and circulation (blood flow through arteries and veins), and are used to treat tremors, angina (chest pain), hypertension (high blood pressure), heart rhythm disorders, and other heart or circulatory conditions.

Many of the people taking auditions use beta blockers of some kind. It's not often discussed, and some people consider it to be a taboo topic. It is not illegal, and it is not immoral. It is also not a performance-enhancing drug.

I've used a beta blocker called Propranolol (Inderal), which was prescribed by my doctor to alleviate the physical symptoms of performance anxiety that I sometimes experience during auditions. These beta blockers take away the shaking of my fingers and quivering of my lips that anxiety causes for me. This makes technical passages and soft playing easier under pressure.

At first, when the physical effects subsided, I experienced some unintended side effects. Without the physical sensations of anxiety in my body, my mind was free to run circles and sabotage all of my efforts! I felt more distracted by my intrusive thoughts and less able to focus. This is what led me to investigate the mental training I mentioned elsewhere in this book. I've also experienced

auditions where I think I may have taken too high a dose, and I was musically catatonic!

Should you use them for auditions? I don't know your medical history. This drug can have harmful side-effects for those with underlying or undiagnosed heart conditions. *This is NOT something for high school students to investigate.*

There are plenty of people who manage their anxiety without the use of medication, and the techniques for doing so—such as exercise, visualization, self-hypnosis, and meditation—are extremely helpful whether you use medication or not. I suggest trying a combination of techniques to manage anxiety before considering the use of medication. During a recent discussion panel hosted by my colleagues in the Detroit Symphony, I was shocked by how many of my musician friends won their jobs without using beta blockers!

Do not get them from a friend or family member who uses them and try them on your own. You should only explore this option under medical supervision.

Information About Beta Blockers

There are a few important things to consider when deciding if or when to try beta blockers:

Types

There are a few different types of beta blockers. Talk to your doctor about the types, what the differences are, and if any might be beneficial for you.

Dosage

Dosage depends on many factors. Based on my height, weight, age, and level of anxiety, I typically take 3–5 milligrams (mg) of Propranolol about an hour before I could possibly have to play and then an additional 3 mg if I advance to a higher round and play the same day (also about an hour before playing). I try not to take much more than that over the course of one day because it can be sedating and have a dulling effect on my musicianship. Be sure you know how many mg are in each pill. You may want to purchase a pill cutter, as you'll have to get good at splitting them into pieces that approximate the dosage you'd like to take. Listen to your doctor and your own body to find the right dosage for your peak performance. Use your mock auditions to help evaluate the effect of a given dosage.

Timing

Using beta blockers takes planning. You can't take them just before walking out on stage to benefit from the effects. Consider the earliest time you might be required to play and then take your dose 45 min to an hour before. If the audition day is delayed and hours pass before you actually need to play, there's no need to re-dose because the medicine will be in your system for about four hours.

Side effects

Some people experience dry mouth when using beta blockers, but this can be managed by staying well hydrated in the warmup room. While the physical manifestations of anxiety may disappear, for some, this might clear a path for unobstructed negative self-talk to enter their mind. In these cases, some mental training needs to be done to address these issues.

Access

You need a doctor to prescribe this medication, so you can't wait until the morning you are leaving and realize you don't have the medication you need. Plan ahead.

Remember: this is a medication (a chemical) that was not designed nor intended to treat performance anxiety. This may not be a good option for you, but I want you to know it exists, and many of your competitors may be using it. Please consult a doctor if you are interested in learning more. Do not get them from a friend or family member who uses them and try them on your own. You should only explore this option under medical supervision.

Audition Protocol

- **Do not** speak to the committee, only to the proctor.

- You can use your own parts, unless they specify you cannot. I'd advise you to use your own parts, but **triple check** the measure numbers they will be asking and the order they will want to hear them. It might be a good idea to glance at the music they provide to see if there are differences in dynamics or articulations, as this is what the committee will be looking at. Most of the time, if there are common discrepancies, they will specify what they want to hear long before the audition. If you have questions, ask at the check-in desk, or ask the audition runner.

- If you mess something up that you can normally play very well, simply ask the proctor if you might try again. Most times, they'll say yes. I don't know if I'd ask more than once, but I've heard people ask to redo more than one excerpt in a round without it counting against them.

- You will have the option to sit or stand. Do whatever you did in your practice! *This is not the time to try something new.* (Plan on the screen being removed for the finals. If you want to stand for the concerto in finals, practice standing). I typically sit when playing anything behind the screen and stand for the concerto if the screen comes down.

- **Do not** contact any member of the orchestra during the audition process (not even if you get cut early). It puts them in an awkward position. Wait until after the audition is over to contact anyone you know.

- **Under no circumstances** should you post anything to social media regarding the audition, including whether or not you advanced, who was in your round or at the audition, how they did, or any other details. *Anything you post can be seen by orchestra members and destroys the anonymity of the process.*

At the Hotel

Stay relaxed and rested. Choose the audition reed. Practice for security and confidence (play technical stuff slowly), but don't overdo it. Continue exercise, warmup, and mental training routines.

The day before you play

- Try to limit practicing to 1–2 hours.
- Do a normal warmup and exercise routine.
- Play technical passages slowly and with relaxation.
- Rehearse mental approach to each excerpt.
- Practice starting each excerpt in the right character.
- Choose THE audition reed and don't play too much on it.
- Limit TV time.
- Read a book.
- Do self-hypnosis/meditation/visualization.
- Have nice meal(s) but no alcohol.
- Get to bed early.

The morning of your audition

- Eat light and be careful of hot food.
- Do your normal warmup on the audition reed.
- Play technical passages slowly and with relaxation.
- Check touchy spots.
- Limit playing to 30–45 minutes.
- Pack your "Audition Survival Kit" in your case.
- Possibly take beta blocker just before leaving hotel
- Plan to arrive one hour before you are scheduled to play.

Notes about the experience

At the Audition / After You Play

Check-In and Holding Room

- Say hello to friends briefly.
- Find a spot for yourself. Put on headphones and get out your book.
- Do not use a group warmup room. They will likely offer you a private room 20 minutes to an hour before you'll play.
- Be nice to everyone but keep chit-chat to a minimum. You'll have time to catch up later. Politely tell them, "I'm just going to stay in the zone for now." They'll get it.
- If you choose to take beta blockers, make your way to the bathroom to take them (if you haven't yet).

Warmup Room

60 minutes until audition

Phone on airplane mode, ear plugs, hand warmers, stretch, yoga, superman pose, read "Direction of Intention", write key character words in order of round, check measure numbers being asked, listen to inspiring music, hydrate, swab, smile!

40 minutes until audition

Start a twenty-minute self-hypnosis or guided meditation, hydrate, swab, smile!

20 minutes until audition

Play a few scales to check reed, don't change it unless something really doesn't work, play along with practice tracks on your phone, use breath builder, start excerpts, read "Direction of Intention", look at photo album, assemble "Stage Kit" (pencil, reed case, cigarette paper, swab, recorder), swab.

5–10 minutes until audition

Press record on recorder, superman pose, listen to opening of concerto, use practice tracks on phone, "Direction of Intention", SWAB.

Delay in audition

Do not warm up too much. Read a book, continue above activities, hydrate, swab, listen to music. Trust yourself. Remember everyone is facing the same challenges.

At the Audition / After You Play

After you play

- Pretend you will have to play again:
  No chit-chatting about how it went. If your friends ask how it went, simply reply, "I think it went well. We'll see what happens."
- Don't ask how other people did.
- Stay focused.

If you have to play again on the same day

- If you have time, go back to the hotel.
- If not, you might have time to at least take a walk.
- Some orchestras will not allow you to leave and may even confiscate your phone for the duration of the audition round, even if you have been cut! Be prepared with low-tech ways to keep your mind occupied (e.g. a good book, puzzles, Rubik's Cube).
- Avoid hanging out with other people. This isn't time to socialize. It's time to stay relaxed, happy, and inspired.

If you have to return to play the next day

- Walk back to the hotel.
- Avoid hanging out with other people.
- Do something to unwind and take your mind off the audition for a bit.
- Exercise.
- Go for a walk, read, or visit a museum (if you need to kill more time).
- Call someone you love.
- Play a bit that evening if you want.
- Do visualization, self-hypnosis, or meditation.
- Have good meal (no alcohol).
- Go to bed early.

Notes about the experience

Direction of Intention Worksheet

Create a one-page Direction of Intention to be included in your audition book and to be read multiple times while in the warmup room waiting to play. This document may evolve as you continue to take auditions and you have experiences with anxieties or intrusive thoughts under pressure. When you do, take note of them, and imagine how your thoughts might better be guided beforehand. Then, update this document for the next audition.

The first section of prompts deal with potential issues you might encounter under pressure. Write one or two short, positive sentences to put yourself in a healthy state of mind with regards to each. Use phrases like, *I will*, *I am*, or *I have*. Avoid the word *don't*. If you find this exercise difficult, imagine coaching someone else—someone you care about and respect! Sometimes it can be easier to help someone else to think in helpful ways than to do the same for yourself.

The second set of prompts are more aspirational and will help you envision the type of musician you want to be.

Once you are finished, assemble the page of phrases you've written and add it to your audition book. Refer to it whenever you feel your thoughts racing. It will become like a mantra and it will keep you calm and focused on what matters.

— EXAMPLES —

Remember to be positive.

Issue: Focusing too much on the outcome.

My healthy mindset:

I WILL BE DETACHED FROM THE OUTCOME, I JUST WANT TO PLAY MY BEST

And make sure to avoid words like "Don't" and "Do not."

Issue: Focusing too much on the outcome.

My healthy mindset:

~~DON'T~~ THINK TOO MUCH ABOUT WINNING!

The brain doesn't register the word "*don't*" and will read "*think too much about winning.*"

Direction of Intention Worksheet

Issue: Focusing too much on the outcome.

My healthy mindset:

_____

Issue: Worrying about what others think of you.

My healthy mindset:

_____

Issue: Experiencing unhelpful mental chatter or lack of focus.

My healthy mindset:

_____

Issue: Dwelling on mistakes.

My healthy mindset:

_____

Issue: Having unhealthy expectations.

My healthy mindset:

_____

Issue: Worrying about high stakes.

My healthy mindset:

_____

Issue: Worrying about being an imposter or not being unique.

My healthy mindset:

_____

Continued on following pages.

Direction of Intention Worksheet

Here are some phrases for you to finish that will remind you of WHY and HOW you do what you do as a musician. Perhaps you've already done exercises like this, so feel free to amend it in any way you see fit. I've included these prompts as a place to start.

Why do you make music?

As a musician, I was put on this planet to _____

How would you like people to describe you as a performer?

I am _____

What do you appreciate about making music?

I want to appreciate _____ *as I play.*

How will you touch the hearts of the audience (committee) when you play?

I want to play with _____ *and* _____ *because they create* _____ *and* _____

That part of your playing you are worried about... describe it as a skill you have.

When I play, my _____ *is* _____ *and* _____

That thing in your playing that you do so well...

I have the ability to _____ *unlike anyone else.*

Describe the best parts of playing music.

This is _____ *and* _____, *and it's what I love to do every day!*

Direction of Intention Worksheet

Finished? Add these sentences to a one page document and experiment by emphasizing key words in your sentences with fonts and sizes. Be creative. Your subconscious mind will thank you for providing some direction when it's "GO TIME".

— SAMPLE FORMAT —

I will be *detached* from the outcome,
I just want to play my best.

Looking to copy mine? I've already given you an example,
now make it your *own!*

Dealing with the mental challenges of this process is often neglected
by many great players.

Do it now!!!!

Work *creatively.*

You can do this. Don't be lazy.

This should be *easy*, and *fun.*

If you're still reading this, what are waiting for?

Get to work!!

Practice Suggestions

Technical/Rhythmic

- Linking
- Penny game
- Mixed up rhythms
- Offsetting the beat
- Short bursts at tempo
- Interleaved practicing
- Relaxation exercises
- Weaning off metronome
- Use BodyBeat
- Record yourself counting mixed meter and play along
- Listen half-speed for issues

Intonation

- Use a drone
- Pitch match on the *TE Tuner*
- Record on *TE Tuner* and see graph
- Playback recording through speakers and watch tuner
- Create a practice track with drone and a score
- Play or record on keyboard to hear intervals
- Sing with drone
- Play warmups with drone

Recording: *What to Do*

- Record 1, listen
- Record group, fix one thing each
- Record half list, listen other half and practice it (rotate)
- Listen to commercial recording, then record and listen to yours
- Record whole list, listen and take notes, and practice

Expressive

- Play along
- Find new recordings
- Record yourself
- Copy favorite recording
- Copy a different recording
- Take on famous musical personality
- Sing phrases out loud
- Sing or play twice as fast
- Pretend you're playing chamber music

Clarinet Pitfalls

- Pressing sound
- Air leaks
- "Twang"– false accents
- Bad pitch in throat tones

Recording: *What to Listen For*

- Are ideas clear?
- Dynamic contrast?
- Any dead spots?
- Character from the first note?
- Is it in tune?
- Is it in time?
- Is it beautiful?

See pages 43–47 for more information.

Keep This in Mind

Sometimes, there is just too much information, and I need clear, concise direction. These bullet points help me remember important goals and helpful thoughts throughout the process.

Strive to be most prepared.

Build dynamic control on soft side.

Do not neglect fundamentals while preparing. This will keep you able to respond to unexpected challenges.

Play for trusted ears. Find people whose feedback helps you move forward.

You should feel like playing an audition is no big deal, but it should sound SPECIAL. Being relaxed and confident shouldn't make it sound boring.

Your unconscious mind is always working. Make it work for you, not against you.

Never give the impression you've hit a limit.

Have in your mind a clear intention at every moment: Keep your phrasing alive and human.

Bring joy to your work and approach with curiosity and creativity.

Remember, everyone is facing the same challenges. If the reeds feel harder on audition day, they will for everyone. If the hall sounds like crap to you, it will to everyone.

Play like you're in a chamber ensemble and communicate musically.

20% of the outcome is not in your control. Accept this fact and do your best to make your 80% the best it can be. Much of the final decision is not in your hands.